# THE RADICAL LIFE OF GRACE

CREFLO DOLLAR

*The Radical Life of Grace*
ISBN-13: 978-0-9994515-0-2


Published by:
Creflo Dollar Ministries
P.O. Box 490124
College Park, Georgia 30349

# CONTENTS

# INTRODUCTION

Something so supernatural begins to happen when you take the time to behold Jesus. When you behold Him, the Spirit of God accepts responsibility to change you into the very image that you behold! Anything you do to try to initiate change on your own will be futile; you will only learn the rhythm of the flesh instead of the rhythm of grace.

One of the greatest issues amongst the body of Christ right now is spiritual blindness—being blind to what Jesus has already accomplished. Think about what it must be like to be saved, but blind. Think about what it must be like to be a Christian, going to church because you love God, but you're blind. You're working to get forgiveness because you don't know that, two thousand years ago, Jesus settled that. Now, if you can get your eyes opened to this grace, you can receive what's already been made available. You'll find out you have an inheritance and that God's not mad at you. He's not even in a bad mood where you're concerned. He didn't kill your family member, and He didn't cause that car wreck. He didn't cause anything bad that happened in your life.

I used to think living the Christian life was hard. Later on, I discovered that living the Christian life is *impossible* if you try to live it without Christ. You need Jesus to live this life. When your eyes are opened to grace, you're gonna receive something that's already been made available. You'll get a hold of the inheritance that's already been set aside for you.

You hear people say, "Oh, I preach the Gospel," in religious church, but I don't know about that. The Gospel is not just preaching the whole Bible. Somebody might say, "The Gospel is the Good News," but there's some bad news in the Bible, too! So, precisely, what is the Gospel? It's unmerited love, unmerited favor. The apostle Paul tells you precisely what the Gospel is: *"But none of these things move me, neither count I my life dear unto myself, so that I might finish my course with joy, and the ministry, which I have received of the Lord Jesus, to testify the* ***gospel*** *of the* ***grace of God****"* (Acts 20:24; emphasis mine). He tells you, here, precisely what the Gospel is: the Good News about the grace of God.

I thought the Gospel had been preached everywhere. In going around the world, I've discovered that the Gospel has not been preached as I thought it was. Preachers proclaim, "I preach the Gospel," so I've got to say this pretty boldly: if you're not preaching the grace of God and the Good News about this grace, you're not preaching the Gospel. If you're not preaching the Good News about this unmerited, unearned favor of God, you're not preaching the Gospel. The Gospel is the Grace of the God. The Gospel is the Grace of Christ. The Gospel is Jesus, who is full of grace and truth. *Grace* is the truth that will make men free. If you're blind to that, then you've got to ask yourself: what is it that you cannot see? What are you missing?

One of the Latin meanings of "religion" is a return to bondage, and we certainly don't want to return to bondage! This whole deal of constantly attending church and hearing that you're gonna have to do *this* in order for God to do *that*; or you're gonna have to do *this* for *this long* in order for God to be able to do what you need; or if you want God to be good to you then—bless God—you're going to have to be good is just absolutely wrong! Yes, there was a time when that was true, but that time is not now! If we don't understand how vital it is to know what has been accomplished and what has been made available to us through Jesus, then we'll continue to carry ourselves in a religious manner.

This revelation of grace has totally revolutionized my life. It has tenderized me. It has caused me to enter into a rest. It's delivered me from fear, condemnation, guilt, and shame. I used to beat myself up every time I wasn't the flawless, perfect preacher. If I said something wrong, I'd beat myself up. If I didn't pray enough, I'd beat myself up. If I missed time reading the Bible, I'd beat myself up. I would beat myself up because I thought this was what I needed to do to qualify to walk in God's blessings. It was never enough in my eyes for it to be satisfying to Him. I could never seem to pray enough, to make enough confessions, to read the Bible enough, to study enough, to walk in faith enough. I thought in order for me to walk in the blessings, I had to perform. So, when my performance level was down, I felt like God wasn't going to bless me or that my love for Him was going to be in question—that things wouldn't happen or the anointing wouldn't happen. *I* just drove *myself*. It was a driven life instead of a directed life.

I thought I needed to do this. I had been taught that you need to pray for an hour a day and that you need to fast. God interrupted me and asked, "What are you doing?" I

FROM THE DESK OF

# DOLLAR

CREFLO DOLLAR

Dear Sarah,

I pray that this letter finds you blessed and overcoming in all things that concern you (Psalm 138:8).

Hebrews 13:9 says, "Be not carried about with divers and strange doctrines (teachings). For it is a good thing that the heart be established with grace..." I will never forget the day that God asked me to become a student of grace. Understanding grace has empowered my life for tremendous change. My heart is established with an understanding of God's unearned favor. I'm at peace, in love with Jesus, and free to live as the righteousness of God.

If you have become a student of grace, you've probably experienced some of these wonderful changes and much more. I'm so encouraged when I read the countless testimonies from people all over the world who tell their story of how grace has changed and impacted their lives. Satan knows that when people understand grace they will be empowered to change.

Hebrews 4:15 informs us that Satan comes immediately and takes away the Word that was sown in our hearts. How? By causing persecution, affliction, or tribulation in areas of your life. The apostle

Paul declared that Satan persecuted him because of the abundance of revelation on the subject of grace (2 Corinthians 12:7).

Child of God, I believe with all my heart that it is the will of God for me to preach the Gospel of Grace all over this world through television, and every available voice. I trust God for His favor and provisions to remain on television, to continue to take the Gospel of Grace to the world. I also trust that you will continue to partner with me in preaching the Gospel of Grace through the airwaves. Your consistent financial and prayerful support is the weapon we need to get the job done. Together, we can give an understanding of grace and empower people to change worldwide. If the message of grace has impacted your life as it has impacted my life, then help me preach the Gospel of Grace to the ends of the earth and establish the hearts of many through this unmerited, unearned, undeserved favor of God. Together, we can do it—we can and will get the job done. Agree with me now, that we have more than enough money to preach the Gospel on television every day until Jesus returns.

Thanks for hearing my heart.

Your Best,

Creflo Dollar

P.S. For your love gift of any amount, I would like to send you my new 316-page book, which has not been released, called ***The Radical Life of Grace***. Let this book convince you that partnership can change this world for Jesus.

We love you!

That they will walk in the authority of God

said, "I needed to fast and pray so I can be more anointed. I heard if you are going to be anointed, you have to spend time with God and you have to fast." Then, the Lord said, "You're already anointed. You're trying to qualify for something I've already qualified you for. *I'm* the one who called you." So that's it. . . you only do what you know to do. That's what I was taught to do. That's what I was trained to do, so that's what I did; but at the end of it all, I still had these questions. Something deep down inside was saying, "I'm missing something. What is this that I'm missing?"

Before I received the revelation of grace, I was frustrated. I knew that something was missing in our revelation of faith, healing, and deliverance. I was frustrated because I would work harder to try to get the promises of God, but my hard work wasn't producing the way I thought it would produce. In the middle of carrying my own guilt and condemnation, the Word of the Lord came to me, and God asked me, "Would you become a student of grace?" I said, "Yes, I'll become a student of grace."

I didn't know too much about grace except what I had already preached at that time. As I began to investigate, I had one question after another question, after another question, after another question. I started on a journey of grace because I was at the perfect place for it. I was at a place where I didn't know what else to do. When you finally get to a place where you have tried everything you know to try, that is when you are ready for grace. Grace changed my whole life. It took me from trying to work for God's love to *receiving* His love.

When people understand grace, they will be empowered to change. So, this book is my opportunity to take you through some things I know will be a blessing to you, to show you how to stop working for God's love and simply receive His love. I'm going to show you how to live the radical life of grace.

# CHAPTER ONE
# THE RELEVANCE OF GRACE

What does it mean to be relevant? Simply put, it means to be connected to the matter at hand. It doesn't mean you lose your identity as a Christian and who you are called to be in order to be relevant. As a Christian, it is inevitable that you will face trials, temptations, and tests of all kinds, things that will try to threaten the positive blueprint for your future that God has promised you in His Word. When you understand the relevance of grace, your connection to it, and its power in your life, you realize you are powerful and full of God's ability. Grace is the good news that God has equipped us with the power to overcome every challenge with which we are confronted. Allowing this to be a significant, relevant truth in your life will cause you to approach life differently.

Jesus didn't die just to forgive you of your sins so that you could go to heaven. He died to set you free from *everything* that binds you and keeps you from living a life of victory over sin, sickness, depression, mental and emotional defeat, and a host of other things that are born out of this fallen world system. His blood provided deliverance from every type of addictive thought, habit, or behavior. It provided deliverance from sickness and disease. It is through His grace that we are able to lay hold of the benefits of what He has done for us.

Now, in order to really experience the fullness of what Jesus has done for you, you are going to have to resolve some things. You are not going after God to heal you, deliver you, or provide for you; these things have already been done. Isaiah 53:4, 5 says, "*Surely he hath borne our griefs, and carried our sorrows: yet we did esteem him stricken, smitten of God, and afflicted. But he was wounded for our transgressions, he was bruised for our iniquities: the chastisement of our peace was upon him; and with his stripes we are healed.*" We *are* healed. This is where a lot of people are missing it. God is not answering prayers for things that He has already done. If you are experiencing physical sickness, the prayer is not for God to heal you, but instead thanksgiving for your healing by faith, through the grace of God. This is the attitude of receiving from the finished works of Christ rather than begging for Him to do something.

First Peter 2:24 says, "*Who his own self bare our sins in his own body on the tree, that we, being dead to sins, should live unto righteousness: by whose stripes ye were healed.*" Again we see that the work was done over 2,000 years ago on the cross. If you were healed in Isaiah 53 and you were healed in First Peter 2, then you are healed right now! The key is to receive the tense in which the healing was completed. You're not praying for healing, you're praying from an already healed place and expecting your body to line up with that truth.

When you believe in the finished works of Jesus, your actions will align with that belief. You will see results in your life, both on an internal and external level. In Mark 2:1-12, a man was brought to Jesus for healing. His friends were so confident in Jesus' ability that they tore the roof off the house where Jesus was holding a gathering, just to get the man into His presence. Jesus saw their faith, forgave the man's sins, and spoke a word to him that moved him to get out of his sickbed and walk. The forgiveness of his sins dealt with the unseen spiritual matters of the heart, and the physical healing confirmed to the crowd that Jesus' authority was legitimate. He verified the work of grace that had happened inwardly in the man's life by allowing the religious leaders to see an outward manifestation.

## THE AUTHORITY IS OURS

As believers, we have the same power and authority that Jesus had. The works He did bore witness to the Father. What this means is that Jesus was the express image of the Father's love, power, and ability in walking, breathing, human form. Works and miracles backed up the words Jesus spoke, and God will also work miracles through our hands when we come into agreement with the power of His grace. The Scriptures let us know that physical signs will accompany the works that we perform as believers. Things like speaking in tongues, casting out devils, healing the sick, and raising the dead are all confirmations of who we are in Christ. The signs that follow a Christian include healing, wholeness, prosperity, and salvation in its fullness. This is all part of our inheritance as kingdom citizens.

The grace of God provides everything we need in this life and the next, but faith takes what grace has made available to us. When God is the most significant aspect of our lives and everything we do is centered around Him, it propels us to move and act in ways that reflect what grace has accomplished. Living this way is the key to walking in signs, wonders, miracles, and a victorious, abundant life.

# STUDY QUESTIONS

1. What does relevance mean? ______________________________

______________________________

2. What happens when you understand the relevance of grace? ______________________________

______________________________

______________________________

______________________________

3. Grace is the good news that ______________________________

______________________________

______________________________.

4. Why did Jesus die for you? ______________________________

______________________________

______________________________

______________________________

5. True or False: A believer who is sick should ask God to heal them.

6. True or False: You have already been healed.

7. Why did Jesus forgive the sick man's sins *before* he was healed? ____________________

____________________________________________________________

____________________________________________________________

____________________________________________________________

8. True or False: You have the same authority as Jesus.

9. What are some of the signs that accompany a believer's walk with God? __________

____________________________________________________________

____________________________________________________________

____________________________________________________________

10. ______________________________ takes what grace has made available to us.

# ANSWER KEY

1. to be connected to the matter at hand
2. You realize you are powerful and full of God's ability.
3. God has equipped us with the power to overcome every challenge we are confronted with.
4. to set you free from everything that binds you and prevents you from living a life of victory
5. False
6. True
7. because He wanted to deal with the inward condition of the man's heart, first, thus making his outward healing a demonstration to unbelievers of His power to forgive sins and also heal
8. True
9. healing, wholeness, prosperity, casting out devils, speaking in tongues, raising the dead
10. Faith

**SCRIPTURE REFERENCES**

Isaiah 53:4, 5

1 Peter 2:24

Mark 2:1-12

# CHAPTER TWO
# THE PROMISE OF WHOLENESS

When something is relevant to you, it has meaning and connection in your life. When it comes to grace, the questions every believer must ask themselves are, "How is grace connected to life itself?" and "How is it significant and relevant when I still see circumstances in my life that are challenging my faith?" God is not only relevant in matters of the afterlife; He is relevant in *every* area of life. He wants to be intimately involved with what you have going on and He wants you to partake of everything that belongs to you.

Salvation is much more than just "fire insurance" or the assurance of an eternal life in heaven after you die. So many Christians live defeated lives on the earth, never realizing their full potential or accessing the many benefits and blessings that come with a relationship with Jesus Christ. Sure, they are heaven-bound, but they are still "under" the circumstances of life instead of being on top of them. God's grace is just as relevant on the earth as it is in heaven and it is vital that we not limit our relationship with God simply to providing a way out of hell. Through the shedding of His blood, Jesus has perfected everything that concerns us. This is the complete salvation reality that He wants us to experience in this life.

God's love has many components and is an active and powerful force in our lives. The first and most significant aspect of this love is that it is sacrificial. Jesus died for our sins, to deliver us *now*, not at some undefined point in the future. The truth is, we need Jesus every day and in every way. Galatians 1:4, *NLT*, says, "*Jesus gave his life for our sins, just as God our Father planned, in order to rescue us from this evil world in which we live.*" Not only did Jesus shed His blood, He did it to deliver us from every kind of evil we could possibly encounter or experience in life. That's right! *Every* kind of evil. This is not to say that the devil won't come against us, because he will, but when Jesus lives in us, we possess a supernatural ability to overcome Satan that those who do not know Him do not possess. This is why it is so important to show the world why Jesus is so necessary to living a successful life. He died to save and deliver all of mankind. He is just waiting for you and me to receive our salvation in its entirety.

In light of what Jesus has done for us, let's examine exactly what salvation entails. Again, salvation is not just being born again. The word salvation comes from the Greek word, *sozo.* This word, when translated, means wholeness, healing, soundness, and preservation. It basically encompasses all the finished works of Jesus. It is the all-encompassing peace and wholeness that restores, preserves, and saves. It is the salvation package that came to you by grace.

Some people find it really difficult to receive God's free gift of grace. Religion paints the picture of a harsh God who demands our effort in order to release His blessings and goodness to us, but this is simply not true. Think back to when you were a child at Christmas time. Do you remember the gifts that were under the Christmas tree? Did you have to do something for your parents to give you those gifts? Did you have to work to earn them? Most of us who experienced the blessing of gift-giving as children know that our parents simply gave those gifts because they loved us and wanted to see us happy. That is the heart of a loving parent. The same is true with our heavenly Father. He desires His children to be happy and to experience the best He has to offer. That's why He sent Jesus, the greatest gift of all!

## YOUR SALVATION PACKAGE

Salvation is a package that includes much more than just being rescued from hell after you die. It is the power that saves from sin, but it also manifests as many other things in the life of a Christian. The key is not to neglect what the blood of Jesus has done for you. When you acknowledge and believe what the blood has done, it will manifest. Salvation delivers, protects, and provides for us in this present world, *right now.*

A great example of this is the account of Jairus' daughter, whom Jesus healed. Mark 5:22, 23, *NLT*, says, "*Then a leader of the local synagogue, whose name was Jairus, arrived. When he saw Jesus, he fell at his feet, pleading fervently with him. 'My little daughter is dying,' he said. 'Please come and lay your hands on her; heal her so she can live.'*" Further down in the chapter, the little girl was completely restored through Jairus' faith in Jesus' ability to heal. This type of healing is yet another manifestation of salvation.

Deliverance is also a part of your divine benefits package. Jesus demonstrated this through the casting out of demons, which was an integral part of His ministry. In Luke 8:36, those who saw Jesus heal a demon-possessed man confessed how He had performed the miracle. After Jesus ascended to heaven, the disciples ministered salvation as they continued the work of Jesus on the earth. Acts 14:8-10 gives an account of how a lame man who had never walked a day in his life heard the Word of God, believed, leaped up, and started walking. He had faith in the salvation that Jesus brought.

## FAITH IS THE ACTIVATOR

In order to experience any of the benefits of salvation, you must have faith. It is the connector to and currency of heaven. Jesus performed many acts of healing and deliverance, and the common denominator between all of the people He healed was that they *believed.* In Luke 6:8-10, He healed a man's withered hand. The same power that saved you and me healed the man, and it was the man's faith that connected him to the grace necessary to be made whole in his body. When you are in Christ, you have a blood-bought right to be saved, forgiven, born again, delivered, and made whole.

Jesus also had mercy on and healed lepers (Luke 17:11-19). They were cleansed when they obeyed and did what He told them to do. All of them went to show themselves to the priests, but only one of them returned to give thanks. Jesus told this man that it was his faith that made him whole. He said the same thing to the woman with the issue of blood who was healed because she acted on her belief that if she could just touch Jesus' garment, she would be healed (Matthew 9:20-33; Mark 5:25-34; Luke 8:43-48). Her healing was immediate as a result. Her faith made her whole.

## WHOLENESS IS YOURS IN CHRIST

Whenever there is something in your life that needs to be restored, you have a blood-bought right for it to be restored, not halfway, but fully. What is it in your life that needs to benefit from your salvation? God's will is for His children to be completely brought into a state of wholeness and He has given you everything you need to access it. This salvation package has a restoration component for everything missing, broken, or stolen, from your health to your finances.

Take time every day to remind yourself that Jesus released His wholeness to you when He took your sins (2 Corinthians 8:9). In order for God to get you what you needed, Jesus had to become broken. He had to become sin, sickness, lack, and every other thing that is under the curse. When Jesus completed His redemptive work, there was nothing missing or broken in His life and, when you are in Him, you automatically partake of the same wholeness. However, experiencing this total life salvation depends on you renewing your mind to what salvation is.

The blessings of the Lord make us truly rich and there are no sorrows attached to the things God gives us (Proverbs 10:22). Being rich in God makes us whole spiritually, physically, emotionally, mentally, financially, relationally, and in every other way. Taking time daily to meditate on the Word of God and remind yourself of His promises is the path to actually experiencing this salvation package. It doesn't matter what things look like, you are whole if you are in Christ. When you received Him as your Lord and Savior, you were restored in the spiritual realm. That is the realm from which all blessings flow. When the salvation of God becomes more real to you than your natural circumstances or physical condition, you will begin to see things change. Your heavenly Father wants you to live an abundant life. Fill yourself with the Word of God so that you can release your faith for the deliverance, healing, and restoration that is encompassed in your divine salvation package. The blessing on your life makes you whole!

# STUDY QUESTIONS

1. True or False: Deliverance is available to us right now.

2. What has Jesus done through the shedding of His blood? ____________________

    ____________________

    ____________________

    ____________________

3. True or False: Although the benefits of salvation are available to all, not everyone will experience them.

4. What is *sozo?* ____________________

    ____________________

    ____________________

    ____________________

5. We obtain God's grace by:

    A. praying for it.

    B. doing good deeds.

    C. receiving it by faith.

6. True or False: God really cares about your happiness and well-being in life.

7. Salvation manifests as:

   A. healing.

   B. deliverance from evil.

   C. forgiveness of sins.

   D. all of the above.

8. You will begin to see things change in your life when the ____________________ becomes more real to you than ________________________________________.

# ANSWER KEY

1. True
2. perfected everything that concerns us
3. True
4. The Greek word from which salvation is translated. It is an all-encompassing peace and wholeness that restores, preserves, and saves.
5. C
6. True
7. D
8. salvation of God; your natural circumstances or physical condition

**SCRIPTURE REFERENCES**

Galatians 1:4, *NLT*
Mark 5:22, 23, *NLT*
Luke 8:36
Acts 14:8-10
Luke 6:8-10
Luke 17:11-19
Matthew 9:20-33
Mark 5:25-34
Luke 8:43-48
2 Corinthians 8:9
Proverbs 10:22

# CHAPTER THREE
# IMAGINATION AS A TOOL OF WARFARE

As a Christian, it is inevitable that you will face trials, temptations, and tests of all kinds. The good news is that God has equipped us to overcome every challenge with which we are confronted. Everything going on in the natural realm begins in the spiritual realm. However, when we are fighting spiritual battles, we should hold fast and never forget the lessons we learn from studying the Scriptures. The imagination is a God-given tool and is one of our most powerful weapons. No other creation has the ability to create things through thoughts or an "image-maker." We have the power to make whatever we visualize and pray about a physical reality. Regardless of what others may think or say, when we combine the imagination God gave us with faith, there is no obstacle or adverse situation that can stop the eventual manifestation of our dreams.

In this world, there are two realities that are operating simultaneously at every moment: the kingdom of darkness and the kingdom of God. They are in direct opposition to one another. As believers, we are constantly being bombarded with assaults on our minds from the kingdom of darkness. This battle is a contest for the souls of men, constantly attempting to draw them away from the truth of God's Word. Because of this, we must employ spiritual weaponry in order to overcome the mental and spiritual onslaughts of the enemy against us.

Second Corinthians 10:3-5 says, "*For though we walk in the flesh, we do not war after the flesh: (For the weapons of our warfare are not carnal, but mighty through God to the pulling down of strong holds;) Casting down imaginations, and every high thing that exalteth itself against the knowledge of God, and bringing into captivity every thought to the obedience of Christ.*" This passage of Scripture is dealing with something that is vital to the success of every believer: the mind and the images that we allow to shape our minds. The way you think is the key to your success or failure; everything begins there. This Scripture talks about casting down imaginations. That is the place we have to start when it comes to dealing with the manifestation of certain situations and circumstances in our lives, especially if we want to change those things.

For most of us, all we have ever heard about imagination has been negative. Using your imagination to create the life you desire is often associated with New Age thinking, but it is actually a biblical concept that is fundamental to the Christian life. With that being said, it is still not something that is taught much in church. Considering that the imagination may be one of the most powerful weapons in our spiritual arsenal, it is something that needs to be addressed. The gift of the Holy Ghost is second to none, but this area that God created and gave us called the imagination could actually be our greatest asset if we'll understand it and not neglect putting it to use.

The imagination is what sets us apart from every other creature. Now when we talk about casting down imaginations, we are talking about thoughts and mindsets that go against the Word of God. Instead of meditating on them, cast them down. If you don't cast these types of thoughts down by declaring what God's Word says, those things will manifest in your life because the imagination is just that strong. When used in line with the Word of God and in tandem with spiritual principles, it can bring into existence things that God placed in your heart.

There is probably no other Bible story that better demonstrates the power of the imagination than the account of the building of the Tower of Babel. Genesis 11:1-6 says:

> And the whole earth was of one language, and of one speech. And it came to pass, as they journeyed from the east, that they found a plain in the land of Shinar; and they dwelt there. And they said to one another, Go to, let us make brick, and burn them thoroughly. And they had brick for stone, and slime they had for morter. And they said, Go to, let us build us a city and a tower, whose top may reach unto heaven; and let us make us a name, lest we be scattered abroad upon the face of the whole earth. And the Lord came down to see the city and the tower, which the children of men builded. And the Lord said, Behold, the people is one, and they have all one language; and this they begin to do: and now nothing will be restrained from them, which they have imagined to do.

These people visualized a great tower that would rise to the heavens. It was because their imaginations were already building it that God knew it would not be long before the physical manifestation of it would be a reality. Because of this, He had to interrupt their plan. Even though they had not completed the tower, they had visualized it in their mind's eye and in the eyes of their hearts. Their imaginations had removed any limits they had in their minds.

Your imagination will work the same way for you. If you can see yourself doing it, all the necessary resources will show up. When you operate in the authority of your image-maker, you can literally create the things you want to see manifest in your life. Visualize them and add your faith to that image by applying God's Word to it and speaking it into existence. This is a powerful form of spiritual warfare that will get results every single time.

### MEDITATION: THE KEY TO ACTIVATING YOUR IMAGINATION

God has a vision of victory and success for us but our cooperation is needed for it to come to pass. This is where meditation on the Word comes into play. Joshua 1:8 gives some powerful instruction on meditation when it says to meditate on the Word day and night so our way can be made prosperous. We are to study the Word and think about it constantly so that we can apply its teachings to our lives. This is what leads to our success. Utilizing the imagination properly starts with meditating on the

Word of God until we can form a clear picture in our minds of what we see the Word activating or bringing to pass. It is through our consistent meditation that we become rooted and grounded in the truth of the Word. Then, we cannot be moved, similar to a plant clipping that develops a root structure when it constantly stays in water. The Word will take root and cause us to grow spiritually when we are constantly sustained by the living water of the Gospel.

Meditating on the Word of God is actually the most important and consistent practice a believer should have in their life, outside of reading the Bible. It is one thing to read the Scriptures, but it is another thing to actually ponder and "chew" on those Scriptures until they begin to nourish and shape your thinking. Meditation is not sitting somewhere and emptying your mind of all thought. Quite the contrary, it is the act of focusing on the Word with laser-beam intensity. It is the process of turning the Word of God over in your mind until it becomes an integral part of your thinking and begins to transform you. It is to mutter and ponder the Scriptures until they actually come alive to you and begin to speak to you in a way that is specific to your life and situation. Meditation is more than just reading the Bible; it activates your imagination so that the Word's promises move from the pages of the Bible into your life.

When you meditate on the Word of God to the point that it begins to go down deep into your mind and heart, the weapons of the devil will not be able to succeed against you. In this way, meditation and imagination work hand in hand to form a powerful barrier against Satan's mental attacks. Isaiah 54:17 secures this promise, "*No weapon that is formed against thee shall prosper; and every tongue that shall rise against thee in judgment thou shalt condemn. This is the heritage of the servants of the Lord, and their righteousness is of me, saith the Lord.*" The Word promises that anyone speaking against you in judgment will be proven wrong. You will have peace and victory as your heritage. This is the result of consistent meditation.

Remember that no matter what you do, you are going to have opposition that will try to keep you from focusing on the promises of God and the positive picture you have created in your mind of your life's outcome. The devil is not going to just roll out a red carpet and allow you to envision a future that is full of the promises of God without a fight. He is going to do everything in his power to stop that from coming to pass, including making suggestions and injecting thoughts to contradict what you have set your mind to accomplish. This is where your tenacity in casting down wrong thoughts and imaginations comes in. Jesus said that in this world you would have opposition, but to take heart because He has overcome the world (John 16:33, *NLT*). It is important to see victory at the end.

Satan has no business winning in any area of your life, but it is up to you to use the spiritual weapons that God has given you to maintain your position of victory on a day-to-day basis. Speaking and meditating on the Word of God and casting down imaginations that oppose the picture God has given you in His Word are your keys to winning in spiritual warfare and enforcing the victory that Jesus made available to you. Use your imagination to cause your destiny to materialize and unfold right before your eyes. Reject anything that does not line up with the wonderful plan God has outlined for you in His Word. Your heavenly Father has given you the keys; don't neglect to use them!

## STUDY QUESTIONS

1. The imagination gives us the power to ______________________________.

2. The enemy bombards our minds with opposing thoughts for the purpose of ______

   ______________________________.

3. True or False: The way you think is vital to your success or failure in life.

4. True or False: Using your imagination to create your reality in life is a fundamental Christian concept.

5. What sets human beings apart from other creatures? ______________________________

   ______________________________

   ______________________________

   ______________________________

6. Why did God have to interrupt the building of the Tower of Babel? ______________

   ______________________________

   ______________________________

   ______________________________

7. You can literally create the things you want to see manifest in your life by ______

______________________ and ______________________________.

8. What is the first key to utilizing the imagination properly? ______________

______________________________________________

______________________________________________

______________________________________________

9. True or False: Meditation should be an integral part of every believer's life.

10. Meditation is:

   A. emptying your mind of all thoughts.

   B. chanting.

   C. focusing on the Word of God, muttering it, and turning it over in your mind.

# ANSWER KEY

1. make whatever we visualize and pray about a physical reality
2. drawing us away from the truth of God's Word.
3. True
4. True
5. Humans are the only creation that has been given the gift of imagination.
6. because He knew that nothing would be restrained from the people because of their imaginations, and a tower built to heaven was not His will.
7. visualizing them; adding your faith to that image by applying God's Word to the vision and speaking it into existence
8. meditating on the Word of God until we can form a clear picture in our minds of what we see the Word activating or bringing to pass
9. True
10. C

**SCRIPTURE REFERENCES**

2 Corinthians 10:3-5

Genesis 11:1-6

Joshua 1:8

Isaiah 54:17

John 16:33, *NLT*

# CHAPTER FOUR
# SALVATION: THE PACKAGE DEAL

Most believers know what it means to be saved, at least from a basic understanding of the fact that accepting Jesus Christ as your Lord and Savior means not going to hell after you die. However, there is much more to being saved than just that. When we look at the entire salvation package that Jesus made available to us through His death on the cross and resurrection from the grave, we see that the animal sacrifices made in the Old Testament were a foreshadowing of what Jesus would do much later. The difference is that, under the Law of Moses, the blood of animals was used to cover up the people's sins, but the blood of Jesus *completely obliterates* our sins. Jesus was the perfect sacrifice for all time, completely washing away our sins and removing them from the mind of God. When you really grasp the magnitude of what Jesus did on the cross, it will revolutionize your life. The salvation of God is powerful.

In order to really take advantage of the complete salvation package, you have to understand that God is the God of the here and now, not just the God of the afterlife. This means that salvation for a believer involves every aspect of our lives on this earth, as well as our lives in eternity with Jesus and the Father. Salvation is much more than "fire insurance" as most people think. Religion puts all the focus on what happens after you die, but it is much more than that. The Greek word from which salvation is translated, *sozo,* also means wholeness, soundness, and peace. It is a promise of wholeness in your life, right here and right now. Jesus' blood was shed on the cross for us so that we could experience total life prosperity right here on the earth. His blood washes away our sins so that we no longer have to be tormented by them. We can live a life of spiritual freedom because Jesus set us free from the law of sin and death and gave us liberty in our souls (the mind, will, and emotions). We can also have freedom in our bank accounts, health, relationships, and more.

## THE PERFECT SACRIFICE

You may have heard the phrase "All roads lead to God" at some point in your life. While this idea sounds perfectly reasonable, especially with so many religions and beliefs which people follow, it simply isn't true. This may sound harsh, but the truth often challenges the predominant way of thinking in the world. The truth is that Jesus is the only way to the Father, and the only way to achieve salvation. He is really the only way to have lasting peace or wholeness in your life. Instead of looking at this as a put-down toward other beliefs, it can be looked at within the framework of who Jesus is, what He did for us, and why what He did for us is the only way the salvation package could be secured for mankind. He was the perfect sacrifice on our behalf, the only sacrifice that was and is able to obliterate sin's power in a person's life. No other person who walked the earth was able to do this, and no other belief system or practice can accomplish this. It is why He, alone, is qualified to be the one, true way to eternal life with God.

As mentioned earlier, the practice of making a sacrifice for sin was taking place long before Jesus came on the scene. As far back as the Old Testament, the understanding of a naturally depraved inward human condition that would bring about the judgment of God was an integral part of the Israelite community's life and practices. There was a need for blood to be shed in order to deal with it. There was something about sin that moved people to have an awareness of two things: 1. Sin was a problem that needed to be dealt with or else there would be consequences. 2. Something had to be sacrificed in order to absorb the consequences of sin so that the members of the community would not suffer for it. Sacrificing animals was implemented as the way to deal with sin and keep the people from being destroyed. Amazingly, it also gives us a picture of why Jesus' sacrifice of Himself was so necessary.

Galatians 1:4, *NLT*, says, "*Jesus gave his life for our sins, just as God our Father planned, in order to rescue us from this evil world in which we live.*" This Scripture shows us that it clearly was God's will for Jesus to give Himself for our sins. Just like the animals of the Old Testament sacrifices were necessary to atone for the sins of the people, Jesus' sacrifice of Himself enabled our sins to be completely wiped out once and for all time, not just covered or atoned for. He was the perfect sacrifice because He was perfect and without sin, but then *became* sin for us. He was God operating as a man in this earth, showing us how to live in a way that pleases the Father. He had no flaws and was without fault of any kind. Only *He* was qualified to be such a perfect sacrifice for mankind.

Jesus went to the cross to save us from eternal death and to rescue us from the evils of this present world. This is essentially what salvation is. Think about how many evils we face on a daily basis living in this fallen world. In heaven, there is no sickness, disease, death, destruction, or evil forces coming against us and sabotaging our lives; but here on this earth, we face all of these things. Jesus died so that we could walk in the same overcoming power that He did when He was here. When we receive Him as our Lord and personal Savior, we come into relationship with Him. Our awareness of our identity in Him and our obedience to the Word of God infuses us with the strength necessary to be victorious in life. His blood delivers and sanctifies us, not just in the future, but right now.

Healing and deliverance from evil are just two of the benefits that can be found in the salvation package. Jesus died on the cross so we can be righteous and free from the power of sin. Before becoming born again, a person is subject to his or her sinful nature and its impulses. At best, they can try to exercise willpower in order to stop doing certain things, but that willpower can only last so long before they will return to their behavior. This is because as sinners, or those without Christ, they are under the dominion of the devil and part of his kingdom. When you are in Christ, you have the ability to overcome; you are no longer subject to that old nature because it no longer resides in you. As a new creation in Christ, you are subject to the law of the spirit of life in Christ Jesus, not the law of sin and death (Romans 8:2). Jesus died so that we could be made righteous and dead to sin. He also died so that we could be healed physically, emotionally, and mentally (1 Peter 2:24). These salvation package benefits are available to all who have received Jesus Christ, but they hinge on our belief in Him.

## GOD'S SALVATION FROM PAST TO PRESENT

Even under the Law of Moses, God's salvation was present and gave us a type and shadow of what was to come through Jesus' sacrifice on the cross. For example, in the Old Testament, the priests did not focus on the sinful man who brought the sacrifice, but rather on the sacrifice itself. The animal was the focus of everything because it was that animal sacrifice that would provide the atonement for sin. The same thing is true today. When we accept Jesus, who intercedes for us, God doesn't see our sins, He sees only Jesus, our high priest who bought eternal redemption for us through His blood (Hebrews 9:11, 12). God doesn't even look at our sins when we are in Christ. He only looks at what Jesus has done and, as a result, our sins are wiped out. Jesus is the *only* one who can ensure our sins are obliterated so that nothing stands in the way of our relationship with the Father.

Another example of the sacrifice of Jesus being foretold is found in Numbers 21:8 when God told Moses to make a serpent on a pole and said that anyone who looked at the serpent would live and not die. That serpent on a pole was actually a foreshadowing of Jesus. It represented Jesus on the cross. The only ones who were healed were those who believed what God said and looked at the serpent. Jesus, Himself, referred to the serpent that Moses made in the wilderness, *"And as Moses lifted up the serpent in the wilderness, even so must the Son of man be lifted up"* (John 3:14). Like those who looked at the serpent, anyone who looks upon Jesus and believes will have eternal life.

## FOCUS ON THE WORD

In order to experience the benefits of our salvation firsthand, we must always focus on the Word of God. We should meditate on it until it gets deep down into our minds and hearts. Jesus has already finished everything that needed to be done to ensure our salvation. By keeping our focus on the Word, we actually keep our focus on Him. He is the one who perfects our faith and completes the work that He started in us when we received Him into our hearts. When we continually choose to behold Jesus, the Spirit of God living in us will gradually transform us into His image (2 Corinthians 3:18).

So how do we practically "behold" Jesus? By meditating and reflecting on God's truths contained in His Word. Doing this will make us prosperous, wise, and successful. We also behold Jesus by visualizing ourselves already receiving and possessing every benefit of the salvation package which Jesus has provided for us. We behold Him by choosing to use spiritual weapons found in the Word of God to fight battles and overcome the devil. We cast down negative thoughts and imaginations that do not line up with the Word. We behold Jesus by relying on His power, alone, to enable us to win in life.

Salvation is available to all who receive it and involves our finances, relationships, health, deliverance, and well-being. You can receive Jesus Christ as your Lord and personal Savior today and access every benefit of salvation. All it takes is a heart that believes in the finished works of Jesus and a willingness to remain focused on the Word of God. Take advantage of the victory that Jesus has secured for you on this earth, as well as the future of an eternity with Him in heaven!

# STUDY QUESTIONS

1. True or False: There is more to being saved than just not going to hell when you die.

2. What is the difference between the animal sacrifices of the Old Testament and Jesus' sacrifice on the cross? ______________________________

______________________________

______________________________

______________________________

3. Salvation is the promise of ______________________________.

4. Animal sacrifices were made in the Old Testament for the purpose of:
   A. atoning for the sins of the people.
   B. ensuring eternal life.
   C. changing the sin nature of mankind.

5. True or False: It was God's will for Jesus to sacrifice Himself for the sins of mankind.

6. ______________________ and ______________________ are two benefits that can be found in the salvation package.

7. True or False: When you are in Christ, you are no longer subject to the power of sin.

8. True or False: God does not see your sins once you are in Christ.

9. In order to experience the benefits of salvation you must ______________________________________________________________________.

10. We practically behold Jesus by:

    A. meditating on the Word of God.

    B. visualizing ourselves possessing the promises of God.

    C. walking in our spiritual authority.

    D. all of the above.

# ANSWER KEY

1. True
2. Animal sacrifices atoned for man's sin, but Jesus' sacrifice obliterated man's sinful nature and sin's power over a person's life.
3. wholeness in your life here on the earth, as well as after you die
4. A
5. True
6. Healing; deliverance from evil
7. True
8. True
9. always focus on the Word of God
10. D

**SCRIPTURE REFERENCES**

Galatians 1:4, *NLT*

Romans 8:2

1 Peter 2:24

Hebrews 9:11, 12

Numbers 21:8

John 3:14

2 Corinthians 3:18

# CHAPTER FIVE
# HOW TO EXPERIENCE REAL LIFE TRANSFORMATION

When we receive Jesus Christ as Lord and Savior, we receive a complete spiritual overhaul. True conversion gives birth to an entirely new spirit and an infusion of eternal life that cannot be undone. Many believers do not experience the fullness of the life God intends for them because they have not renewed their minds to who they really are in Christ. Real life transformation happens when the issue of identity is settled. Though the spirit of a person is recreated instantly at the moment he or she receives Christ, the mind must be renewed to this new spiritual reality in order to lay hold of what rightfully belongs to us as sons and daughters of God.

Second Corinthians 5:17 lets us know that we have been made into new creatures spiritually. The born-again spirit is a species of being that has never existed before! When a person gets born again their spirit is recreated, but the spirit is only one-third of the human system. Man is a spirit; he possesses a soul; and he lives in a physical body. The body gives us the physical equipment to move, live, and have authority on the earth. Unfortunately, even as born-again people, we tend to know and relate more to our physical bodies than we do our recreated spirits. The soul includes the mind, will, and emotions, but it is not the same as the spirit. All three components were designed to function in alignment with the Word of God.

The new identity of a person who has been born again is very real. If you are in Christ, your old spiritual state has been completely obliterated. Many believers still operate from a sin-consciousness because they do not know who they truly are in Christ. You are no longer a sinner, but you have been made the righteousness of God by faith in Jesus Christ, alone. In fact, the "sinner" you used to be doesn't even exist anymore. Real transformation in every area of your life is going to be based on whether you believe you have truly become a new creature in Christ Jesus.

The idea that if you continue to sin after salvation, you are still a sinner, is actually not true. A person could be born again and house a recreated spirit but, because he or she has not renewed his or her mind, the same behaviors and mindsets that ruled their life before Christ still function. This does not, however, mean that their spiritual condition of righteousness has changed or that they are a sinner. A sinner, by biblical definition, is one who has not received Christ.

First Thessalonians 5:23 says, "*And the very God of peace sanctify you wholly; and I pray God your whole spirit and soul and body be preserved blameless unto the coming of our Lord Jesus Christ.*" We are truly brand new creations when we receive Jesus! However, the soul and the body must be brought into subjection to the born-again spirit. God created the human system to be dominated by the spirit, not the unrenewed soul or the body. We are the ones who are responsible for renewing our minds with the Word so that our thinking and emotions line up with our recreated spirits. Once the mind, will, and emotions come into agreement with the Word, the body will begin to line up. When we allow our spirits to lead us, God will always take us in the direction we need to go and we will get where we need to be. When the Word of God becomes our guidance system, we will always come out on top, no matter what situations we face.

## WHAT DO YOU BELIEVE?

Whether you realize it or not, what you believe about yourself is going to be the key to the results you get in life as a Christian. This is why knowing your identity is so important. Right-believing produces right-living, but wrong-believing produces wrong-living. When we don't have the right belief about ourselves, we cannot truly walk in repentance. In fact, real repentance is changing what we believe about ourselves to line up with the truth of who we are in Christ. Repentance is not simply being sorry about bad behavior; it is changing your mind about your identity. It is choosing to no longer identify with the tag, "sinner," and instead choosing to embrace the truth of being made righteous. A person's behavior will change when they change how they think about themselves and what they believe about themselves.

Keep in mind that no matter what happens, what you do is not an indicator of who you are. What you do is the result of who you *believe* you are. You produce the works of righteousness when you believe you are righteous. The issue of behavior is actually secondary to the inward belief about who you are. Real transformation happens when we settle the issue of identity within ourselves. The truth is that the recreated spirit is identical to God. In Christ Jesus, we are righteous and God sees us this way, even when we miss the mark. Change of belief comes first, then transformation follows.

So, how does transformation through change of belief happen? Through focus. Whatever you focus on is what you give strength to, which is why it is so vital to focus on what the Word says about you rather than focus on who you used to be. Colossians 1:27, 28 says, "*To whom God would make known what is the riches of the glory of this mystery among the Gentiles; which is Christ in you, the hope of glory: Whom we preach, warning every man, and teaching every man in all wisdom; that we may present every man perfect in Christ Jesus.*" The glory mentioned in this Scripture refers to the manifested promises of God found in the Word. What is this mystery that is rich in manifestation? It is Christ in you! We have been sealed with the Holy Spirit and are now seated with Jesus in heavenly places (Ephesians 1:13; Ephesians 2:6). Christ in us is our hope, our right to earnestly expect manifested Word to show up in our lives. For this reason, Jesus should be our focus. We should constantly give strength to who we are in Christ, not who we used to be.

Ephesians 1:17 says, "*That the God of our Lord Jesus Christ, the Father of glory, may give unto you the spirit of wisdom and revelation in the knowledge of him.*" God wants our focus to be strictly on Him and in Him. Wisdom is knowing what to do even when you don't know what to do in your own ability; it is a manifestation of grace.

There is a tremendous amount of power available to believers, but we have to lock our focus onto Jesus in order to tap into it. The benefits of being in Christ include having spiritual authority and the right to command. We don't have to put up with anything from the devil because we have already overcome him in Jesus. Renewing our minds to who we are enables us to walk in this power.

The Gospel is so powerful because it qualifies even the worst sinner. Religion tells people they are not included because they don't line up with the idea of what a perfect Christian should look like, but the Gospel of Grace invites *all* to be included in the abundant life Christ died for us to have. When we know our identity and settle who we are in Him, we can walk in the healing, deliverance, prosperity, and good life that He has designed for us. There is no condemnation to those who are in Christ Jesus (Romans 8:1). Our new nature is our new identity. Embrace it in order to experience transformation that has a lasting impact on your world.

# STUDY QUESTIONS

1. True or False: Righteousness can be "undone" when we sin.

2. Why do many believers never experience the fullness of what God has for them?

   ________________________________________

   ________________________________________

   ________________________________________

3. When a person gets born again, their spirit is ____________________.

4. The soul includes ______________________________.

5. True or False: If you have been born again, your old nature is completely obliterated.

6. True or False: If you are saved and continue to sin, you are a sinner.

7. How was the human system designed to operate? ____________________

   ________________________________________

   ________________________________________

   ________________________________________

8. What is the glory in Colossians 1:27, 28 referring to? ______________________

______________________________________________

______________________________________________

______________________________________________

9. What are the benefits of being in Christ? ______________________

______________________________________________

______________________________________________

______________________________________________

10. True or False: The Gospel qualifies the worst sinner.

# ANSWER KEY

1. False
2. They have not renewed their minds to who they are in Christ.
3. recreated immediately
4. the mind, will, and emotions
5. True
6. False
7. to be dominated by the born-again spirit
8. the manifested promises of God in our lives
9. having spiritual authority and the right to command
10. True

**SCRIPTURE REFERENCES**

2 Corinthians 5:17

1 Thessalonians 5:23

Colossians 1:27, 28

Ephesians 1:13

Ephesians 2:6

Ephesians 1:17

Romans 8:1

# CHAPTER SIX
# THE FOUNDATION OF RIGHTEOUSNESS

## HOW TO BE FREE FROM SIN-CONSCIOUSNESS

The idea that as a Christian you will never sin is simply erroneous. Missing the mark is an inevitable part of life, even for the most disciplined believer. We all have moments where we succumb to our flesh and fall short of God's instructions. Being a Christian does not mean living a perfect life. In fact, it is in our weakness that God's grace goes to work on our behalf, ultimately giving Him the glory when we come through the situation. No matter what is going on, however, one thing we must not do is allow guilt and condemnation to overtake us. Sin-consciousness will actually cause you to sin more and remain in that state of mind. On the other hand, when you are righteousness-conscious, you won't find yourself in bondage to sin any longer. Understanding who you are in Christ Jesus is the key to living free from sin-consciousness.

Hebrews 10:22 says, "*Let us draw near with a true heart in full assurance of faith, having our hearts sprinkled from an evil conscience, and our bodies washed with pure water.*" So many believers live miserable lives of guilt and condemnation because they have an evil conscience. An evil conscience is a conscience that is more aware of sin than righteousness; and it eventually forms the foundation of guilt, even though the blood of Jesus has already taken care of the penalty for sin. When one has this type of consciousness, he or she has an extremely difficult time accepting God's eternal forgiveness through Jesus and is unable to let go of their shortcomings. Consequently, they find it difficult to forgive others. Constantly reminding yourself of your wrongs keeps that mindset intact and cuts you off from receiving the benefits of God's grace. Doing this also strengthens a performance-based mentality in which one believes that their good deeds can put them in right-standing with God. The truth is that in order to forgive ourselves and receive God's forgiveness, we have to first believe that Jesus Christ has already made us right with God. Only then will we be free to live a life of grace instead of living with sin-consciousness.

## RECEIVE CHRIST, RECEIVE RIGHTEOUSNESS

There is only one way to purify your mind from an evil conscience and it is by accepting Jesus Christ as your Lord and Savior. Have you ever met someone who is constantly repenting for every little thing they do? This person feels perpetually guilty for some reason or another, whether they actually sinned or not. When they do miss the mark they may experience deep condemnation and fear God's wrath and judgment. They can never really receive forgiveness because they believe that God is mad at them every time they mess up. Having sin-consciousness is pure torment.

The core belief that keeps sin-consciousness going is the belief that God needs us to perform up to His standards in order for Him to accept us. Unfortunately, all this does is foster a law-based mindset. When we are thinking according to the old covenant, we depend on our own self-effort instead of trusting Jesus' ability and His finished works. Dead works are an attempt to earn right-standing with God. The problem is that nothing we do in our own ability will ever qualify us for righteousness. There is only one person who accomplished this task—Jesus—and this is what makes Christianity so unique. Only Jesus has the ability to recreate a man's spirit and completely eradicate the sin nature. Jesus is alive and well, and He is forever making intercession for us before the Father (Hebrews 7:25). Through Jesus, we can live free from the guilt, shame, and condemnation of sin.

Religion always tries to convince us that it takes more than just the blood of Jesus to get rid of the stain of sin, but the blood is the most powerful cleansing agent that exists (Hebrews 9:13, 14). It cleanses the mind of sin-consciousness and the "dead works" mentality. To receive this free gift of righteousness there has to be a true heart-belief that we have been made righteous through Jesus Christ, not through our works.

Nothing stops faith in the life of a believer more than sin-consciousness. Because everything in the kingdom of God requires faith, it is impossible to lay hold of Jesus' finished works when you are burdened by guilt. First Timothy 4:1, 2 says, "*Now the Spirit speaketh expressly, that in the latter times some shall depart from the faith, giving heed to seducing spirits, and doctrines of devils; Speaking lies in hypocrisy; having their conscience seared with a hot iron.*" A seared conscience is a mindset that has progressively gotten worse as it relates to sin-consciousness, and is completely overtaken by awareness of sin, guilt, shame, and condemnation. As a result, the cycle of sin, guilt, shame, and condemnation continues, trapping them in misery day after day and leading to more of the same. The seared conscience happens when we repeatedly miss the mark and then feel condemned because we didn't measure up. It can take a toll on any person and keep them from receiving God's blessings.

The other side of the spectrum is to live a grace-based life that is led by the Holy Spirit. Living the life of grace requires belief-effort, not self-effort. Yes, there is effort required in believing; it is not just mental assent. Believing involves casting down thoughts, renewing your mind, laboring to enter into rest, and considering the promise more than you do the circumstance. All of these things require resisting the opposing forces of contrary situations and the enemy's tactics. When we believe, we practically demonstrate our faith in God and His Word. We have to push back against the resistance that challenges us; however, this is the only type of action we are to take as new covenant people. We are not supposed to be striving or working to make God accept us.

With that being said, the reason guilt is so dangerous to a believer's mind and heart is because it has the potential to completely undermine your faith and destroy your sense of worth and acceptance from God. It causes a person to become angry, bitter, obsessed with their past mistakes, and subject to blame others for their actions. The Law of Moses was given to show people their sinfulness and expose their guilt (Galatians 3:19, *AMPC*). The purpose of the Law of Moses was not to bring about righteousness.

Another side effect of guilt is condemnation. People who feel condemned all their lives believe they are worthless and they can't receive unconditional love from God. Satan will jump on the bandwagon and amplify these feelings even more, causing them to spiral further into despair. He is the accuser of the brethren and will not miss any opportunity to point an accusatory finger at us (Revelation 12:10). This can lead a person into deep depression and even suicide. It can also cause them to become even more rebellious, which can be deadly.

## GETTING FREE

Freedom from sin-consciousness can only be achieved by allowing the blood of Jesus to purge us of dead works. When we try to achieve what Jesus has already done through self-effort and performance, instead of believing, we keep ourselves trapped in sin-consciousness. While we are actually free from sin's dominion, many times it takes time to become healed from a seared conscience. The first step to living a life of grace is that we have to believe we are forgiven and forgive ourselves. We must forgive ourselves, even if we don't think we deserve forgiveness. This is so important because if we don't forgive ourselves we won't be able to forgive others. When we feel we don't deserve forgiveness, our actions will be driven by our guilt and shame. The problem is that doing the "right" things to try and make ourselves worthy of forgiveness never resolves a guilty conscience. Jesus is the only cure for a conscience that is ridden with guilt and condemnation.

Understanding the new covenant and your position as a believer under the dispensation of grace is critical. The power of sin is dead without the law. Romans 7:6-8, *AMPC*, expounds:

> But now we are discharged from the Law and have terminated all intercourse with it, having died to what once restrained and held us captive. So now we serve not under [obedience to] the old code of written regulations, but [under obedience to the promptings] of the Spirit in newness [of life]. What then do we

> conclude? Is the Law identical with sin? Certainly not! Nevertheless, if it had not been for the Law, I should not have recognized sin or have known its meaning. [For instance] I would not have known about covetousness [would have had no consciousness of sin or sense of guilt] if the Law had not [repeatedly] said, You shall not covet and have an evil desire [for one thing and another]. But sin, finding opportunity in the commandment [to express itself], got a hold on me and aroused and stimulated all kinds of forbidden desires (lust, covetousness). For without the Law sin is dead [the sense of it is inactive and a lifeless thing].

Getting free from sin-consciousness is absolutely vital in a believer's life. Taking on the weight of sin is destructive to your spiritual life and will drive you further into a place of unworthiness and shame. Because the law was given to bring awareness to sin and man's need for a Savior, when you try to live under the law it will actually keep sin alive in you. This is not God's plan for those who are born again. Jesus has set us free from the law and, as believers, we now live under the covenant of grace. Under the law, we were obligated to do good so that God would bless us, but under grace it is all about what Jesus has done; we are no longer a part of the equation. Sin has no dominion over us now that Jesus is Lord of our lives.

Living free from sin, guilt, and condemnation is the distinguishing mark of those who have gotten a revelation of the Gospel of Grace. Faith is rendered ineffective when sin-consciousness is allowed to remain. The result is that guilt then becomes your taskmaster and begins to control your life, robbing you of the beauty of the life of grace. Through Jesus we have been completely set free from the bondage of sin-consciousness. When you receive that you are the righteousness of God, you will start acting righteously and will begin to walk in the liberty that comes from the covenant of grace.

# STUDY QUESTIONS

1. Why do so many Christians live a miserable life of guilt and condemnation? ______
______
______
______

2. True or False: When you don't forgive yourself it is difficult to forgive others.

3. What needs to happen in order to forgive ourselves and receive God's forgiveness? ______
______
______
______

4. True or False: Jesus purifies us from sin-consciousness.

5. What are dead works? ______
______
______
______

6. What is a seared conscience?

   A. a conscience that is progressively focused on sin

   B. a reprobate mind

   C. a renewed mind

7. True or False: Grace gives us the freedom to sin.

8. Guilt causes a person to become ____________, ____________,

   ____________, and ____________.

9. Why was the Law of Moses given? ____________________

   ______________________________

   ______________________________

   ______________________________

10. True or False: The law activates sin in our lives.

# ANSWER KEY

1. because they do not accept God's eternal forgiveness through Christ
2. True
3. We must first believe that Jesus has already made us right with God.
4. True
5. the works we do depending entirely on human ability instead of trusting Jesus' ability
6. A
7. False
8. angry, bitter, obsessed with their past mistakes; subject to blame others for their actions
9. to show people their sinfulness and expose their guilt
10. True

**SCRIPTURE REFERENCES**

Hebrews 10:22

Hebrews 7:25

Hebrews 9:13, 14

1 Timothy 4:1, 2

Galatians 3:19, *AMPC*

Revelation 12:10

Romans 7:6-8, *AMPC*

# CHAPTER SEVEN
# UNDERSTANDING THE FOUNDATION OF RIGHTEOUSNESS

When someone is building a house, the most important part of the structure is the foundation. In order for that building to withstand the elements and the stress that the house will inevitably endure, the foundation must go deep and the framework must be flexible, yet strong. Just like a house must be built on a strong foundation, so must our spiritual lives be built on the foundation of righteousness. This is really the first layer of a foundation that will result in multiple blessings being released in our lives. Too often we allow self-righteousness to dictate how we relate to God, ourselves, and others, but God's righteousness is the only thing that lasts. By understanding the redemptive work of Jesus Christ we can gain a strong understanding of our right-standing with God and experience His finished works.

Before anything else, Christ is the foundation for a Christian's life. When we are in Christ, we possess His wisdom, righteousness, sanctification, and redemption. First Corinthians 1:30, 31 says, "*But of him are ye in Christ Jesus, who of God is made unto us wisdom, and righteousness, and sanctification, and redemption: That, according as it is written, He that glorieth, let him glory in the Lord.*" All of these spiritual attributes are not the result of anything good that we have done, but they belong to us strictly because of what He has done. Since we are in Him, everything that He possesses is ours.

Psalm 11:3 says that if our *"foundations be destroyed, what can the righteous do?"* Spiritually speaking, if we let religion and the world's philosophies destroy our foundation of righteousness, our whole spiritual house will collapse. Religion and the Law of Moses cannot secure righteousness, which is why it is so dangerous to try and live by these things. God's grace was given to us so that we could be wise builders who rely solely on the finished works of Jesus. Our spiritual houses are built progressively as one person lays a foundation and another builds. When it is all said and done, there is no better foundation to build your life on than Christ. He is the unshakeable foundation that enables us to endure when life's challenges show up. We should never be ashamed of the Gospel of Grace because it is the power of God bringing salvation for everyone who believes (Romans 1:16).

### ON SOLID GROUND

Allowing Jesus to be your sure foundation requires faith that sometimes falters in the beginning (1 Corinthians 3:10, 11). Even the disciples struggled with the true identity of Jesus and what He truly meant in their lives. Though they had walked with Him during His earthly ministry, they still didn't have a full revelation. Jesus asked them once who they thought He was and Peter answered correctly because he had received a direct revelation from the Father in heaven.

Matthew 16:13-18 says:

> When Jesus came into the coasts of Caesarea Philippi, he asked his disciples, saying, Whom do men say that I the Son of man am? And they said, Some say that thou art John the Baptist: some, Elias; and others, Jeremias, or one of the prophets. He saith unto them, But whom say ye that I am? And Simon Peter answered and said, Thou art the Christ, the Son of the living God. And Jesus answered and said unto him, Blessed art thou, Simon Barjona: for flesh and blood hath not revealed it unto thee, but my Father which is in heaven. And I say also unto thee, That thou art Peter, and upon this rock I will build my

church; and the gates of hell shall not prevail against it.

Jesus presented His very own disciples with critical questions designed to see if they really knew who He was. Sadly, none of them could answer because they did not have a personal revelation of Him being the Son of God. Peter, formerly known as Simon Bar-jona, was the only one who received a direct revelation about Jesus straight from the Father. From that moment on, Jesus called him Peter, which means "a fragment of rock," and declared that the rock of revelation of who Jesus was would be the foundation upon which the body of Christ would be built.

This type of direct revelation is what every believer should have when it comes to knowing who Jesus is. It is one thing to mentally agree that Jesus is the Son of God, but it is another thing to know within the depths of your soul that His identity as the Son of God is responsible for making you righteous, apart from anything you could ever do on your own. A working revelation of Jesus is what makes a believer's identity completely impenetrable by the enemy. When you know who Jesus is, it will change your entire perspective, enabling you to walk in the confidence of who you really are because you know who He really is. Jesus is the one who empowers you to live a victorious life by grace. When He lives in you He will completely revolutionize how you view yourself and what you are capable of. The Son of Love, Himself, will empower you to love others unconditionally, forgive, and live a life of faith. A believer who is completely immersed in a revelation of who Jesus is is an unstoppable force!

What Jesus does for us is immeasurable and unfathomable to the natural mind. He gives the free gift of righteousness and the abundance of grace, which empower us to live the kind of dynamic, faith-filled life that He lived on the earth. Romans 5:17 says, "*For if by one man's offence death reigned by one; much more they which receive abundance of grace and of the gift of righteousness shall reign in life by one, Jesus Christ.*" The same Word that makes us the righteousness of God gives us the power to reign.

Since righteousness is the foundation of a successful Christian life, what does it mean to be the righteousness of God? First, righteousness is not something we can attain on our own. Righteousness is imparted into your born-again spirit the day you make Jesus Christ the Lord of your life. It is not something you earn, qualify for, or achieve through self-effort or good works. It is a spiritual force and a spiritual condition that is inherent to every believer, regardless of your outward behavior. Nothing changes your status of being righteous when you are in Christ, not even when you sin. You are just as righteous after you sin as you are before, although God doesn't want us to sin. When we do miss the mark, we can take comfort in knowing that our position in Christ never changes. This should inspire us to allow His righteousness to express itself through us. The believer's responsibility is to renew the mind so that your thinking can change to line up with your new nature. When you get saved, your spirit is born again, but your soul (mind, will, and emotions) remains the same. Each believer must be proactive in the mind renewal process by reading and meditating on the Word of God so that they can gain a new perspective on who they are now that they are born again. This is a lifelong process, not a one-time event, that must be committed to day in and day out.

Perhaps one of the most amazing benefits of being made righteous through Jesus is that you have the right to come boldly before the throne of the Father without a sense of guilt or condemnation for anything you've done in the past (Hebrews 4:16). This means that, even when you sin, you can continue to come to God without reservation. You always have a listening ear with the Father because you are a part of His family through Jesus Christ. In fact, He only sees you through "Jesus-lenses" so you do not have to walk in shame, fear, guilt, or condemnation about anything.

To be *made* righteous means righteousness is imputed to you through no action on your part. You are translated from darkness into the kingdom of God's dear Son through your faith in Him who redeemed you from your sins. This is why trying to do good works to achieve this spiritual state is pointless and futile. Once you become born again, you are instantly made righteous and nothing can unravel your spiritual position. Instead of striving to be made right with God in your own ability, simply receive your new nature as one of Jesus' finished works. When you sin, that is the perfect time to lean into your righteousness rather than running away from God. Have no doubt that God sees you just like He sees Jesus. Confidence in this truth will enable you to continue your walk with God, fearlessly, even when you make decisions that don't line up with the Word. Your confidence is in Jesus, not yourself.

The enemy hinders believers who haven't renewed their minds to the righteousness of God within them by plaguing them with guilt, shame, and condemnation. If you find yourself being overcome by these things, it is an indication that you need to develop in this revelation. Meditating on Scriptures that tell you about your identity in Christ will strengthen your foundation of belief in your new nature and what you possess as a born-again believer.

Hebrews 5:12, 13 says, "*For when for the time ye ought to be teachers, ye have need that one teach you again which be the first principles of the oracles of God; and are become such as have need of milk, and not of strong meat. For every one that useth milk is unskilful in the word of righteousness: for he is a babe.*" So many believers need to be taught and *re-taught* the basic foundational principles of Christianity, including righteousness. Spiritually speaking, a person is a babe in Christ if they are unskillful in the Word of righteousness (Hebrews 5:13). Continual study and application of the Word of God in this area will help to bring spiritual maturity to "baby" Christians who need to develop their new identity. There will be many opportunities to grow in righteousness-consciousness, which is why it is so important to grasp it and walk in it.

Every day we will be faced with opportunities to cower in the face of guilt, shame, and condemnation. There is always something from our past, whether it is last year or yesterday, that the enemy will try to use to tear down our identities; but it is our responsibility to build ourselves up in the revelation of who Jesus is and what He has done for us. The foundation of righteousness gives us bold access to the Father and all that is promised in the Word of God. It helps us to remain confident in what we possess, no matter what we have done before or after receiving Christ. When your spiritual life is built on the foundation of the righteousness of God, none of your mistakes or past sins can trip you up or hinder you from moving forward in your relationship with God. Embrace your new nature today and walk in the power that is rightfully yours!

# STUDY QUESTIONS

1. As Christians, the first foundation we must understand is the foundation of ______ ______.

2. True or False: When we are in Christ we have His wisdom, righteousness, sanctification, and redemption.

3. What is the Gospel? ______

   ______

   ______

   ______

4. True or False: All we need in life is grace.

5. Where did Peter get his revelation of who Jesus really was? ______

   ______

   ______

   ______

6. What is a benefit of righteousness? ____________________

____________________

____________________

____________________

7. Why are many believers not walking in victory over the enemy? ____________________

____________________

____________________

____________________

8. True or False: The Word of righteousness brings spiritual maturity to babes in Christ.

# ANSWER KEY

1. righteousness
2. True
3. the good news and the grace of Christ
4. True
5. It was revealed to him directly from the Father in heaven.
6. It enables you to stand before God without shame, fear, guilt, or condemnation.
7. because they are not skillful in the Word of righteousness
8. True

**SCRIPTURE REFERENCES**

1 Corinthians 1:30, 31
Psalm 11:3
Romans 1:16
1 Corinthians 3:10, 11
Matthew 16:13-18
Romans 5:17
Hebrews 4:16
Hebrews 5:12, 13

# CHAPTER EIGHT
# RIGHTEOUSNESS BY FAITH

Understanding the righteousness of God is something that is vital to getting things to work in your life as a Christian. We simply have to understand that, under the grace of God, our works are not relevant; Jesus' finished works make the difference. When you don't know who you are in Jesus, you will be subject to every attack of the enemy to get you in a place of guilt and condemnation. As a result, you will not be able to exercise your faith in God's love or promises to you, and you will definitely not be able to walk in the power that God has given you to do the works that Jesus did. God has given every believer divine authority and we need to know what we are capable of. It starts with a revelation of our righteousness. In Jesus, we are the righteousness of God! Though religion in the church today has become all about self-righteousness, the grace of God is the exact opposite. Because of the blood of Jesus, we have access to untold blessings that need only to be received by faith.

Christians must begin maturing spiritually in the revelation of their righteousness so that they can live the kind of abundant life that God has designed for them. You can be saved for thirty years but, if you are still not skillful in the lifestyle of righteousness, you are still a babe in Christ. It is time for us to be weaned from self-righteousness so that we can grow up into our true identities. Hebrews 5:12, 13 says that when we are unskillful in the word of righteousness we are still operating from a place of spiritual immaturity. For this reason, the foundation of righteousness must be taught again. It truly is one of the most important components of the Christian life.

A basic overview of righteousness is this: Jesus became sin for us so that we could be made the righteousness of God through Him. Second Corinthians 5:21 says, "*For he hath made him to be sin for us, who knew no sin; that we might be made the righteousness of God in him.*" You see, on our own, we could never perform enough righteous deeds to achieve this status. So many believers think that a holy lifestyle is what makes us holy; the truth is that our holiness is only achieved through Jesus, and it is manifested *through* our lifestyle. Righteousness and holiness are internal states of being. Our behavior reflects righteousness because of who we inherently are, not because we are trying to achieve this condition on our own or through how we act. This is the difference between being religious and allowing a thriving relationship with God to manifest through us. When you put self-righteousness out of your life, you also put the law-based way of living out of your life and you invite the grace of God to completely upgrade your way of thinking about yourself.

## RIGHTEOUSNESS THREE WAYS

Your righteousness is going to constantly be under attack, so it is vital that you understand who you are and maintain your position in righteousness. This is when you will see God do all kinds of wonderful things in your life because you know who you are in Him. There are three definitions of righteousness that are a part of the Christian walk: right-standing before God, standing before Him as if we have never sinned, and standing before Him without guilt, shame, inferiority, or fear. Let's explore each of them further.

Right-standing before God is essentially being able to stand before God in the same spiritual state as Jesus, Himself! That may blow some minds but it is the absolute truth for someone who is born again. The reason for this is because when you receive

Christ, your spiritual nature changes. Being born into sin means that you are born in a spiritually defective state. When Adam sinned in the garden of Eden, he became disconnected from the life force of God, his source, and instantly became connected to Satan. His spirit was infused with darkness and the light of God was turned off. As human beings, we are all born into this state because of the sin of Adam, and we all possess the sin nature. However, when you receive Jesus as your Lord and Savior, you are instantly disconnected from Satan spiritually, and re-connected to the Father, just as if you had never sinned (John 1:29). Your spirit is reborn, or recreated, and filled with eternal life. You are a new species of being, spiritually, that has never existed before.

From a spiritual standpoint, you look just like Jesus when you accept Him as Lord and Savior of your life. Now, your mind, will, and emotions are *not* recreated. Therefore, they must be renewed, daily, by meditating on the Word of God so that your thinking aligns with your new nature. But spiritually, you are a clone of Jesus Christ and, because of that, the Father sees you as such. He sees you as holy, righteous, and filled with His nature (Colossians 1:22, 28).

The second definition of righteousness is the ability to stand before God as if you have never sinned. To an unrenewed mind, this concept is almost unfathomable. How can someone who has just sinned stand before God as if it never happened, when it actually *did* happen? The answer is simple: Jesus. When Jesus was nailed to the cross, He bore the sins of mankind and took the full penalty for our sin. He received in His body and spirit the full burden of sin and its consequences. After He died, He went to hell where His spirit suffered the pains of hell and the entire wrath of God. He absorbed it completely so that we wouldn't have to.

When you accept Jesus into your heart, you receive the benefits of His redemptive work. Because of what He suffered, you no longer have to suffer. Because of His sacrifice, you no longer have to look forward to an eternity in hell. Because He took on the sins of mankind in full, you can stand before the Father as if you have never sinned. Your sins haven't just been covered, they have been kicked out of socket and completely obliterated. Your slate is wiped clean and you have access to the continual flow of His cleansing blood at all times. When you sin, you can simply go before the Father, receive your forgiveness, and keep moving forward. No matter what sin you engaged in, if you are a believer, you are free from the guilt and condemnation associated with it, and the sin nature is eradicated from your spirit. This should boost your confidence as a son or daughter of God.

Finally, righteousness means you are able to stand before God without a sense of fear, guilt, inferiority, or shame. This is a big one because so many Christians walk around perpetually guilty and ashamed for one reason or another. The truth is: there is no condemnation to those who are in Christ Jesus (Romans 8:1). Under the Law of Moses, people lived in constant fear of God and His wrath, and rightfully so. They were under the old covenant, which had a completely different set of guidelines. The priests were the only ones who could even offer sacrifices to God. No one could have an intimate relationship with the Father or come into His presence because they still had the sin nature residing in them. Because of this, guilt, shame, and condemnation were the order of the day. No one could rest easy if they broke any aspect of the law; but the good news of the Gospel of Grace is that, if you are in Christ, you have a new nature and the liberty to commune with God regardless of your shortcomings. You don't have to fear God or His wrath, and you don't have to run from Him. The Father is waiting with open arms for you to approach Him with confidence. Righteousness through Christ Jesus entitles you to full access to God without any sense of inferiority.

## NO MORE SELF-EFFORT

The reason attempting to become righteous through self-effort is futile is because it is like trying to work for something that has already been bought for you. This fundamental principle of righteousness must be embraced and our minds have to be renewed to it. Religion tells you that you have to do more and be more for God to accept you. Then, it condemns you when you fail to live up to those expectations. That's what the Law of Moses did. If we allow the law to serve its purpose, which is to show us our need for a Savior, we will be able to see that Jesus was beckoning mankind to Himself even under the old covenant. We are children of the new covenant and not the old.

Romans 4:1-8 says:

> What shall we say then that Abraham our father, as pertaining to the flesh, hath found? For if Abraham were justified by works, he hath whereof to glory; but not before God. For what saith the scripture? Abraham believed God, and it was counted unto him for righteousness. Now to him that worketh is the reward not reckoned of grace, but of debt. But to him that worketh not, but believeth on him that justifieth the ungodly, his faith is counted for righteousness. Even as David also describeth the blessedness of the man, unto whom God imputeth righteousness without works, Saying, Blessed are they whose iniquities are forgiven, and whose sins are covered. Blessed is the man to whom the Lord will not impute sin.

We can look to the patriarch Abraham to see that righteousness cannot be attained through self-effort. Abraham was made righteous strictly through his faith in God and nothing more. This is a wonderful example of the grace of God at work. Because of our righteousness, God does not count sin against us, but releases us from the burden of it.

Jesus' blood makes it possible for us to access the benefits of righteousness and right-standing with the Father. Even before the foundation of the world, God chose us to be in Him, that we should be holy and without blame before Him (Ephesians 1:4). It is just up to us to receive His invitation. Through Christ, we are presented blameless before the Father. We are perfected not by our own merits, but through Jesus.

So many believers live a law-based life even though they are no longer under the law. As a result, they carry and maintain sin-consciousness in their lives, and are tormented by guilt at every turn. Living under the law as a new-covenant believer is counterproductive to everything Jesus accomplished for you. Romans 3:19, 20 says, "*Now we know that what things soever the law saith, it saith to them who are under the law: that every mouth may be stopped, and all the world may become guilty before God. Therefore by the deeds of the law there shall no flesh be justified in his sight: for by the law is the knowledge of sin.*"

This Scripture is vital for every new-covenant person to truly understand. The law points out everything we have done wrong and highlights our guilt, which is why continuing to live a legalistic life as a believer is not what God wants for us. Trying to achieve righteousness through good works will not accomplish that goal because the law simply brings more awareness to sin. God wants us to be more aware of our righteousness than anything else. Sin-consciousness is damaging to the heart and mind of a Christian, and paralyzes them from being able to boldly do the works that Jesus commanded us to do.

No matter what happens in life, always remember that faith in Jesus alone is what makes us righteous; it is the foundation for a victorious Christian life. We cannot build our faith on our own ability, our own righteousness, or what we deem "good" behavior. Once you believe and receive that you are righteous, not because of anything you have done but because of what Jesus has done, the sky is the limit. Maximize your right-standing with the Father and do great exploits on the earth by receiving the truth about who you are in Christ—righteous as if you have never sinned.

# STUDY QUESTIONS

1. Knowing what we are capable of starts with ______________________.

2. Maturing spiritually is vital because ______________________.

3. A basic overview of righteousness is ______________________
______________________
______________________
______________________.

4. Holiness is only achieved through:

   A. Jesus.

   B. good works.

   C. a combination of both.

5. What are the three definitions of righteousness? ______________________
______________________
______________________
______________________

6. True or False: When you receive Jesus you look just like Him spiritually.

7. True or False: When you receive righteousness you can stand before the Father as if you had never sinned.

8. Righteousness through faith in Jesus entitles you to ______________________________ ______________________________.

9. Living under the Law of Moses results in:

   A. righteousness.

   B. carrying a sin-consciousness.

   C. favor from God.

10. What is the cornerstone for a victorious Christian life? ______________________________ ______________________________ ______________________________ ______________________________

# ANSWER KEY

1. a revelation of our righteousness
2. it provides new and deeper insight into what Jesus has given us
3. Jesus became sin for us, so that we could be made the righteousness of God through Him.
4. A
5. right-standing before God, standing before Him as if we have never sinned, and standing before Him without guilt, shame, inferiority, or fear
6. True
7. True
8. full access to God without any sense of inferiority
9. B
10. Faith in Jesus alone

### SCRIPTURE REFERENCES

Hebrews 5:12, 13
2 Corinthians 5:21
John 1:29
Romans 8:1
Romans 4:1-8
Ephesians 1:4
Colossians 1:22, 28
Romans 3:19-22

# CHAPTER NINE
# LIFE AFTER THE CROSS

The Bible is probably one of the most misunderstood and misinterpreted books that exists, even among Christians. Most of the misunderstandings arise because people do not know the difference between the old and new covenants. Too often we apply old covenant truths to new covenant realities, and the result of this error is spiritually dangerous. We can read the Bible cover to cover but, if we are not understanding the true meaning of what God is saying in the Scriptures, we might as well be reading a fairy tale. Unfortunately, that is exactly what many people think the Bible is—a carefully-crafted fairy tale. In order to really be able to apply the Bible to our lives properly, we must understand that there is a sharp contrast between the Old and New Testaments. The best way to look at it is: "before the cross" and "after the cross." The old covenant, which was based on the Law of Moses, required that man follow the letter of the law in order to be blessed by God. At the same time, there was a curse attached to disobeying the Law of Moses. Under the new covenant, however, we now live under grace. Because of what Jesus did when He shed His blood for us on the cross, we no longer have to fulfill the requirements of the law in order for God to bless us. Knowing what life after the cross looks like is vital for a healthy, thriving Christian life.

Getting the most out of the Word of God isn't just about reading the Scriptures, but it is about how we *understand* the Scriptures. This profoundly impacts how we live our lives and the results we experience. So often Christians incorrectly interpret the Bible or take things out of context. They may not know how the old and new covenants affect the way God deals with people. We must learn how to rightly divide the Word by studying the Scriptures through the lens of God's grace.

This may offend the religious mind, but the reality is that, now that we are under the covenant of grace that was established after the cross, we cannot preach the old covenant and the Law of Moses as the rules by which we are to live. Jesus shed His blood on the cross, becoming the perfect sacrifice for all time. With this in mind, we must ask ourselves if we are seeing things from a pre-cross or post-cross perspective. This will have an impact on how we see ourselves and others, and how we see God and His dealings with people, today.

God doesn't handle people the same way under the new covenant that He did under the old. Many times, when reading the four gospel accounts, we forget that the old covenant was still in effect during Jesus' earthly ministry. It wasn't until He shed His blood on the cross that the new covenant was actually cut with mankind. The law, as described in the old covenant, was what the Jews of Jesus' day adhered to and understood. So when Jesus began to teach during His earthly ministry, He was presenting new-covenant concepts to people who were not yet enlightened to what would come after He died. But that was okay! Jesus was laying the groundwork for the new covenant by introducing the principles of the kingdom of God to the world, even though the Jews weren't ready for it. He paved the way for the covenant of grace to be preached. It would be through this covenant that all people, including those Jews who only knew the law, would have the opportunity to receive salvation.

### THE LAW OF MOSES: A PERFORMANCE-BASED SYSTEM

The Law of Moses, which was the moral and religious standard of the old covenant, was a performance-based system that reflected the "do good, get good" principle

(Deuteronomy 28). This is really important to understand because it is essentially the guiding principle of self-effort-based religion that many Christians adhere to. When we feel we have to work harder, do more, and be better in order for God to bless us, we are still operating under a law-based mindset. Under the old covenant, overlooking even one small area or instruction from the law brought a curse. For this reason, the Jews had to continually offer sacrifices every year to cover their sins. The problem was that these sacrifices never eternally took care of the sin problem; it was more like a temporary fix. The issue of sin needed more than just the blood of bulls and goats.

Thankfully, Jesus introduced a system that relies not on our abilities or efforts, but on the faithfulness of God, alone. Under the new covenant, we no longer have to continually offer sacrifices for our sins like the Jews under the Law of Moses. While the blood of animals atoned for the sins of people under the old covenant, it did not wipe sin out completely. When something is covered, it is not obliterated. However, through Jesus' one-time, perfect blood sacrifice, we have been delivered from the curse of the law. Our sins have been wiped out of God's mind (Hebrews 8:12). We have been eternally cleansed from sin and have received a completely new nature. In addition, we have been delivered from the curse of the law.

Galatians 3:13, 14 says, "*Christ hath redeemed us from the curse of the law, being made a curse for us: for it is written, Cursed is every one that hangeth on a tree: That the blessing of Abraham might come on the Gentiles through Jesus Christ; that we might receive the promise of the Spirit through faith.*" Jesus took the curse on Himself when He was hung on the cross. Because of this, we do not have to worry about becoming cursed when we sin or miss the mark. The price has already been paid for us through Jesus' perfect sacrifice.

Because of Jesus, we are no longer required to earn our salvation through our good works. We are not made righteous because we keep all the rules. In Christ, we are blessed because of *His* obedience, not our own (Romans 5:19). Unlike in the Old Testament, our obedience is simply our *response* to what Jesus has already done, not an action we take to get God to bless us. This idea is a religious one that Christians must renew their minds out of. There are definitely blessings involved with obeying God and there are consequences in this world for disobeying the Word, but our motivation for obeying Him is not to try and earn our way into His approval. Grace and righteousness are gifts from God, gifts we receive because of Jesus, not our own efforts.

The way God set the new covenant up was genius because it is all about what Jesus did for us, which eliminates the tendency to boast about ourselves, how good we are, how well we followed through with His instructions, or how we prayed to get results. Jesus' redemptive work was the great equalizer because it put all of us on a level playing field and relieved us from having to perform in order to get God to accept us. It is an amazing thing to know that we no longer have to bear the burden of trying to perform for God's acceptance!

There are many Christians who have not received this powerful revelation yet, but when it is received by faith, it frees you from feeling that performance-based religion is what impresses God. Jesus paid the ultimate price and, when we are in Him, it is as if we never sinned. That's right! It is as if we never sinned! The Father views every believer through eyes of love and acceptance when they receive Jesus. When we miss the mark, we simply receive the continual flow of Jesus' cleansing blood, and the forgiveness that has already been released to those in Him. Through Him we have righteousness, wisdom, redemption, sanctification, and holiness (1 Corinthians 1:30). We have spiritual blessings which will result in the fruit of the Spirit being expressed through us.

Remember, everything about the old covenant was based on personal effort to fulfill the law and get a positive response from God. For example, there was a requirement to forgive others before God could forgive you (Matthew 6:14, 15; Mark 11:25, 26). However, after the cross, we are taught that we are already forgiven through accepting Jesus Christ (Ephesians 4:32; Colossians 3:13). Under the old covenant, we are commanded to show perfect love to God and others (Mark 12:30, 31), but under the new covenant, we see that God loved us first, therefore we can show that love to others (1 John 4:19). God will never require anything from us that He has not already put in us. We have the ability to love and forgive others because His love lives in us and expresses itself through us. We are empowered through this new covenant to walk as Jesus did. Because He has fulfilled the entire law, even becoming a sacrifice for sin on man's behalf, in Him we are free from the bondage of the law's consequences. Jesus took the penalty on our behalf.

## THE REQUIREMENTS OF FAITH

Keep in mind that before Jesus came, the people did not have the faith that we have today. They only had the law but, because Jesus is the source of our faith, we can lay hold of everything in the covenant of grace. Even the concept of faith under the old covenant was based on the people having faith, first, before they could be blessed. Before the cross, none of Jesus' disciples were born again, and He constantly referred to them as having "little faith;" but in the New Testament, after Jesus death, people's lack of faith was never mentioned. This is because, as believers, the fact that we have received Christ demonstrates that we have saving faith, which is necessary for us to access the grace of God in thc first place. This gives us another clear indication of pre- and post-cross spiritual life.

When your faith seems to waver, always remind yourself that Jesus is the author and finisher of it (Hebrews 12:1-3). Just like Peter when he walked on the water, we should keep our eyes on Jesus and focus only on Him at all times. Before faith came through Jesus, everyone was under the law, but now that faith has come, we are no longer subject to the penalties and requirements of the old covenant. We are saved through faith in Him alone and, as a result, we are now partakers of every benefit of salvation. This is what life after the cross truly looks like for the believer who has an understanding of the new covenant and accesses what grace has made available.

# STUDY QUESTIONS

1. What is the difference between the old and new covenants? ____________________

2. True or False: Knowing what life after the cross looks like is vital to a healthy, thriving Christian life.

3. True or False: How we understand the Scriptures profoundly impacts how we live our lives and the results we experience.

4. The new covenant started:

   A. when the first book of the New Testament was written.

   B. after Jesus shed His blood on the cross.

   C. when the Holy Spirit came on the day of Pentecost.

5. How did Jesus pave the way for the new covenant before He died? ____________________

6. The Law of Moses was a ________________________________________

 system that reflected ________________________________________.

7. True or False: Jesus' one-time sacrifice freed us from all aspects of the curse of the law.

8. Our obedience is a response to ________________________________________

________________________________________

________________________________________.

9. True or False: The idea that God won't forgive you unless you forgive others is a new-covenant concept.

10. ____________________ faith is necessary for us to access the grace of God.

# ANSWER KEY

1. The old covenant was based on man's performance and the new covenant is based on what Jesus has already done.
2. True
3. True
4. B
5. by introducing the kingdom-of-God-way of doing things to people
6. performance-based; the "do good, get good" principle
7. True
8. what Jesus has already done, not an action we take to get God to bless us
9. False
10. Saving

**SCRIPTURE REFERENCES**

Deuteronomy 28
Hebrews 8:12
Galatians 3:13, 14
Romans 5:19
1 Corinthians 1:30
Mark 11:25, 26
Matthew 6:14, 15
Ephesians 4:32
Colossians 3:13
Mark 12:30, 31
1 John 4:19
Hebrews 12:1-3

# CHAPTER TEN
# THE REQUIREMENTS OF TITHES AND OFFERINGS

What does God have to say about money? Is giving tithes and offerings something He requires of Christians today? Are there consequences for not giving tithes and offerings that believers should be aware of? The topic of financial giving is one that tends to bring significant confusion to the body of Christ, particularly when it is tied into a performance-based way of doing things. As we have learned, the old covenant, before the cross, was based on what people had to do *first* in order to receive a blessing from God. After the cross, however, the order was changed. Now the focus is on what Jesus has already done. Jesus obeyed the Father and fulfilled His assignment to die for man's sins. As a result, we are blessed when we receive Him. Under the new covenant, it is Jesus' obedience that secures the eternal blessing, first, *then* our faith in what He did that invites it into our lives. Our obedience is not the same type of requirement as described in the Old Testament. This is not to say that we should not obey God or that there are no consequences for disobedience. His instructions to us for Christian living are for our benefit. Obedience is our response to the finished works of Christ, just like faith, love, and forgiveness are responses. Similarly, financial giving to God is a response to what Jesus has obtained for us, not a requirement.

*So you're saying that believers are not required to give tithes and offerings?* It may challenge your religious mindset, but no, we are not. When we study God's Word (2 Timothy 2:15), especially the New Testament, we see that giving isn't about fearing God's response to us if we don't; it is about learning to trust Him enough with our resources that we become givers (Luke 16:10, 11). When we sow financially, we prove to ourselves that our faith and our trust in God are strong. It builds our faith in Him and His provision even more.

Jesus is ever faithful to provide for our every need. He gives money and resources to those who are givers, and He takes care of His own (2 Corinthians 9:10). After the cross, financial blessings are now a result of what Jesus has already done for us, not what we think we are required to do according to the old covenant. Giving under the new covenant is more about our heart-attitude in response to God's goodness in our lives than it is about trying to get blessed (2 Corinthians 9:7). Through Jesus we are already blessed. We give because we love Him, not because we are required to do so. This shift in perspective releases us from the fear of running out or the fear that we will be punished if we don't pay tithes. Giving financially only sets us up for good because of the principle of seed, time, and harvest. Even more than that, it is an active demonstration of our love for Him and trust in His provision.

Part of the salvation package that Jesus bled and died for includes the financial inheritance that rightfully belongs to us as sons of God. He took our sins upon Himself and exchanged them for His righteousness. Now we are enriched and live abundantly supplied lives (2 Corinthians 8:9). We have a blood-bought right to financial provision because of what Jesus did. When we give, we are expressing our faith in this truth.

Believers should never worry about financial provision or money running out because God promises to take care of us even better than the birds of the air, which neither sow nor reap, and still enjoy the benefits of His provision (Luke 12:24). If He takes care of the animals of the earth with such care and precision, how much more will He take care of those for whom He died and who are now beneficiaries of God's grace? When we trust Him with our finances, we are releasing our faith, which pleases God.

The idea that there is a curse associated with not giving tithes and offerings comes from the Law of Moses. In the book of Malachi, there was definitely a clear consequence for those who did not tithe (Malachi 3:8-11). The people were required to give, first, before receiving God's favor and, in failing to tithe and give offerings, they incurred a curse. God referred to it as robbery. However, that was under the old covenant. The concept of becoming cursed for not giving tithes and offerings is no longer in effect, just like the idea of any sin causing you to be cursed is also null and void. Under the new covenant, we give because we want to, not because we are afraid that if we don't God won't bless us. It is basically a shift from a law-based mindset to a grace-based one. If we give to avoid being cursed, it is fear-based and produces no positive harvest anyway. However, when we give out of appreciation, love, and thanksgiving to God, we are sure to not only experience the joy that comes from engaging in God's system of seed, time, and harvest, but we are also free from fear and condemnation.

# STUDY QUESTIONS

1. True or False: Obedience based on the fear of something bad happening to us if we don't obey is an old-covenant mindset.

2. When we study God's Word we learn to trust Him enough to become ______________________________.

3. Giving under the new covenant is about:

   A. earning God's favor and blessing.

   B. our heart-attitude in response to God's goodness in our lives.

   C. securing a financial future for ourselves.

4. True or False: There is a financial inheritance that belongs to us through Jesus.

5. Financial giving is an act of our ______________________________.

6. True or False: If we don't tithe or give offerings we are under a curse.

7. Why do we give under the new covenant? ______________________________

   ______________________________

   ______________________________

   ______________________________

# ANSWER KEY

1. True
2. givers
3. B
4. True
5. love for God
6. False
7. because we want to, not because we are afraid of what will happen if we don't

**SCRIPTURE REFERENCES**

2 Timothy 2:15

Luke 16:10, 11

2 Corinthians 9:7, 10

2 Corinthians 8:9

Luke 12:24

Malachi 3:8-11

# CHAPTER ELEVEN
# THE SUFFICIENCY OF GOD'S GRACE

Do you know what God's grace really looks like? Do you know why it was released to us? The grace of God is something that must be understood. For so long the concept of grace has been misapplied simply because of a lack of understanding about what it truly is. Grace is more than a religious cliché; it is an actual person—the person of Jesus Christ. The good news of the Gospel is actually the grace of God; there is no other Gospel that we should preach. Grace is the redemptive work of Christ that was completed two thousand years ago through His death, burial, and resurrection. It is the power of God that gives us the supernatural ability to receive every promise in His Word. It is what empowers us to live holy lives. Armed with an understanding of grace, Christians are truly equipped to overcome the world and walk in the victory that has been secured for them.

Reducing grace to a "message" really diminishes the significance of it and takes away from the richness of its revelation. Now, this may challenge some of the religious-minded people out there, but there is actually no other Gospel besides the grace of God. In Galatians 1:1-7, the apostle Paul confirms this point:

> Paul, an apostle, (not of men, neither by man, but by Jesus Christ, and God the Father, who raised him from the dead;) And all the brethren which are with me, unto the churches of Galatia: Grace be to you and peace from God the Father, and from our Lord Jesus Christ, Who gave himself for our sins, that he might deliver us from this present evil world, according to the will of God and our Father: To whom be glory for ever and ever. Amen. I marvel that ye are so soon removed from him that called you into the grace of Christ unto another gospel: Which is not another; but there be some that trouble you, and would pervert the gospel of Christ.

"Gospel" essentially means news that is almost too good to be true. What news is this? It is the unmerited, unearned favor that Jesus bestowed on mankind by coming to this earth, shedding His blood, and paying the price for our sins so we don't have to. Although religion emphasizes righteousness through works over righteousness by faith, this is not what the Gospel is all about. The truth is there is *nothing* you could have possibly done in your own ability to be saved, and there is nothing you can do now to make yourself any more worthy of God's gift of salvation. The only requirement is simply believing in Jesus. His grace, alone, is the source of the empowerment that heals and delivers you. Grace is the source of everything good in our lives. The good news about His grace is the key, central message of the Bible. It must be shared with others.

## RESTING IN THE FINISHED WORKS OF JESUS

Too often, Christians get wrapped up in principles as the basis for everything they do, but applying principles without relying on what Jesus has already done won't get lasting results. We must fully trust in the finished works of Christ alone, not our execution of principles.

Ephesians 2:8, 9 are foundational Scriptures for grasping this concept. They say, "*For by grace are ye saved through faith; and that not of yourselves: it is the gift of God: Not of works, lest any man should boast.*" Notice that Paul says your salvation is a gift from God. The Amplified Bible Classic version of verses 8 and 9 says:

> For it is by free grace (God's unmerited favor) that you are saved (delivered

> from judgment and made partakers of Christ's salvation) through [your] faith. And this [salvation] is not of yourselves [of your own doing, it came not through your own striving], but it is the gift of God; Not because of works [not the fulfillment of the Law's demands], lest any man should boast. [It is not the result of what anyone can possibly do, so no one can pride himself in it or take glory in himself.]

What is Paul saying here? It is that the salvation you received had nothing to do with your good works or self-effort. Your salvation came as a result of unearned and unmerited favor, alone. That's what grace literally is. It is God's willingness to do a favor for us strictly because He loves us, and nothing more. That kind of love is unfathomable! Because of Adam's transgression in the garden of Eden, God decided to do us a favor and save us without us deserving or earning it. He gave us the free gift of salvation. All we have to do is receive it by faith. Because our effort had nothing to do with securing this gift, we can't take any credit for it. Because the responsibility is not on us, and never was on us, we can rest in what God has done. The grace of God is the power that causes the finished works of Jesus to become a reality in our lives.

## EMPOWERED TO LIVE A GODLY LIFE

The instructions God gives us to live for Him seem extremely difficult at first glance, and they truly are if you try to carry them out in your own ability. As a born-again person, you now have the nature of God living in you. You can give birth to the fruit of righteousness because you have the root to that fruit in your spirit. The problem is that your body and your mind did not get born again. For this reason, you must renew your mind with the Word of God.

Second Peter 1:3 says that God has given us all things that pertain to life and godliness through His divine power, which is grace. Because of this, we do not have to rely on our own efforts to live upright lives before God. The root of righteousness that lives in our spirits is alive and, through grace, we have the ability to produce that fruit in our lives. We are able to live in a way that pleases God *through His grace*. Now, grace never empowers us to sin or live according to the dictates of the flesh. Rather, it breaks sin's dominion over our lives. What a relief! We are no longer subject to sin, and we don't have to obey its dictates (Romans 6:6). Faith and grace were never designed to assist you to do things that aren't in agreement with the Word of God. They were only designed to help you appropriate the finished works of Christ.

Grace is also the connection point that enables Christians to lay hold of *every* promise in the Bible. Again, principles can only take you so far. Financial blessings, deliverance, healing, favor, a thriving marriage and family, and more are accessed through the grace of God. Salvation is not just being saved from hell and securing an eternity with Jesus in heaven; it is also about living an abundant life, right now! Titus 2:11 says that this grace has appeared to all men, so it is available to everyone. To receive all that grace has to offer, we must simply believe and receive what Jesus did for us by faith. The more you give your attention to hearing about what grace has made available to you, the more your faith in it will grow.

## NOT ABOUT SELF-EFFORT

So often we try to change people's behavior or our own behavior without realizing that behavior modification is not the answer to pleasing God. He is concerned more with what we believe. The key to right-behavior is right-*believing.* Meditating on the truth of God's grace makes our faith in it grow. This is the key, not trying to change outward behavior through willpower. We are to seek first the kingdom of God by first believing the right things (Matthew 6:33). This adjustment in our beliefs is what will cause our behavior to change. You can't do the things that please God until your beliefs line up with His Word.

Christianity isn't a religion; it's a relationship with Jesus, the Holy Spirit, and His grace. Religion focuses on righteousness through works, but relationship focuses on righteousness by faith in what Jesus did. This redemptive work of Jesus is complete and perfect in every way. It doesn't need anything added to it in order for it to be legitimate. To think you have to add your works to what Jesus has done is simply unbelief, and is the fruit of religion. A relationship with Jesus is the connection to His grace that empowers you in every area of your life.

The Gospel of Grace is so amazing! Since nothing you did qualified you for righteousness, your sin actions can't alter your righteousness once you accept Jesus as your Lord and Savior. As Christians, we miss the mark regularly, and to think otherwise is simply wrong. Even though every sin we commit is not visible or seen by others, we still have shortcomings. The good news is that God already made provision for our sins. Jesus' redemptive work on the cross took care of our past, present, and future sins. We were made righteous through faith in that work alone; nothing can undo this powerful act of grace, not even our own sins. God no longer credits sins to our spiritual accounts because Jesus took the penalty and paid the price for them. God declares the ungodly righteous when they accept Christ, simply because of their faith in Him.

### THE POWER OF GRACE

Isn't it wonderful to know that God's grace has the power to make flawed men and women righteous? That's good news! Abraham is a great example of this. Romans 4:1-5 says:

> What shall we say then that Abraham our father, as pertaining to the flesh, hath found? For if Abraham were justified by works, he hath whereof to glory; but not before God. For what saith the scripture? Abraham believed God, and it was counted unto him for righteousness. Now to him that worketh is the reward not reckoned of grace, but of debt. But to him that worketh not, but believeth on him that justifieth the ungodly, his faith is counted for righteousness.

Justified means declared righteous. Like those who have received Jesus as their Lord and Savior, Abraham didn't obtain his righteousness through the works of the law, through performance, through self-effort, or through keeping any kind of rituals. He did nothing out of his flesh. It was simply the unmerited favor of God. Abraham believed, and heaven said, "You're righteous." If righteousness could be earned, it wouldn't be called a "gift."

Why is the grace of God mandatory for personal transformation? Because every person ever born on the planet is born into sin. The nature of sin was imparted to humanity through Adam. His actions in the garden of Eden made all of us guilty and doomed to an eternity in hell; but Jesus, with His precious love, saved us by grace. As a result, the charges against us were dropped, and the case dismissed by the Father. All of our sins and their consequences were placed on the body of Jesus, who willingly became the sacrifice for sin on our behalf.

## DELIVERANCE FROM SIN

The grace of God is in operation to deliver you from the flesh, which is a way of thinking that goes against the Word of God. This is the battle that every Christian will find himself or herself fighting. The real you, which is your born-again spirit, doesn't sin. In the times when you miss the mark, it is because in that instance you did not win the battle of the mind. The key in all of this is to remain focused on the grace of God. In Christ, you are dead to sin, buried with Him by baptism into death, and raised from the dead by the glory of the Father (Romans 6:2-4). Now, you walk in the newness of life because, when the Father resurrects you, life is imparted on the inside of you. The degree to which we think, believe, and act like who we are in our spirit is the degree to which we will experience the life of Christ in our flesh. In other words, you've got to start acting like the real you and not the old, "flesh" you. This comes through renewing your mind with the Word of God.

Jesus paid the price for every single person in this world to be delivered from their sins and the sin nature. God's grace is completely sufficient not only to deliver us from our sinful nature and give us a new life, but to *keep* us delivered when temptation knocks at the door of our minds. Resting in the finished works of Jesus is the key to living a prosperous, successful, and abundant life. Grace truly is sufficient.

# STUDY QUESTIONS

1. Grace is:

    A. a person.

    B. a curriculum.

    C. a message.

    D. an empowerment.

2. What does "Gospel" mean? ______________________________

    ______________________________

    ______________________________

    ______________________________

3. What is required for a person to receive salvation? ______________________________

    ______________________________

    ______________________________

    ______________________________

4. The grace of God is the ______________ of everything good in our lives.

5. What does grace enable a Christian to do? ______________________________

______________________________________________________________

______________________________________________________________

______________________________________________________________

6. Why is behavior modification not the answer to pleasing God? ____________

______________________________________________________________

______________________________________________________________

______________________________________________________________

7. Christianity isn't a religion, it is ________________________________.

8. Why is God able to not hold our sins against us? ______________________

______________________________________________________________

______________________________________________________________

______________________________________________________________

9. What enables us to be delivered from sin? ____________________________

______________________________________________________________

______________________________________________________________

______________________________________________________________

# ANSWER KEY

1. A
2. news that is almost too good to be true
3. believing in Jesus
4. source
5. live a life that pleases God
6. because God is more concerned about what we believe than behavior modification
7. a relationship with Jesus
8. because Jesus bore our sins on the cross
9. faith in the grace of God

**SCRIPTURE REFERENCES**

Galatians 1:1-7

Ephesians 2:8

Ephesians 2:8, 9, *AMPC*

2 Peter 1:3

Romans 6:6

Titus 2:11

Romans 4:1-5

Romans 6:2-4

# CHAPTER TWELVE
# GRACE REVEALED IN THE NEW COVENANT

If you have ever wondered what the grace of God is all about, you can simply look to the person of Jesus Christ. He is the living, breathing, physical manifestation of grace revealed to the world. The law, which is found in the Old Testament, was given by Moses, but grace and truth came by Jesus (John 1:17). In fact, He came to give us more grace, not more of the law. The Bible is actually a book of covenants. The old covenant foreshadows the grace of God that showed up through Jesus in the new covenant. Christians have tried to understand the old covenant without having a new-covenant perspective. That doesn't work. Without a solid understanding of the new covenant, we will filter all of our understanding about God through the law. The law actually brings condemnation and sin-consciousness into the body of Christ. A revelation of the grace of God as revealed in the New Testament is the key to living a life of absolute freedom from sin.

If you are not sure how the Old and New Testaments intersect, the first step is to understand that Jesus is the link between the two. The cross is the dividing line between the old and new covenants. Only after Jesus died on the cross were we able to move into the new covenant and partake of its benefits. Jesus was a Jewish man born under the law (Galatians 4:4) so that He could redeem the Jews from the law and bring them to the new covenant. That new covenant would eventually extend to Gentile, or non-Jewish, people. The whole purpose of extending this covenant to non-Jews was to provoke jealousy in them for the purpose of bringing them to Christ (Romans 11:11).

The whole purpose of the law was to bring man to the end of himself, to show him that righteousness is not attainable through good works or self-effort, only through faith in Jesus. The law was never given to make us holy, but to stir up the guilt and condemnation that is associated with sin. In this way, it would reveal to people that their sin could not be dealt with through the law. This is why trying to keep the law to become holy or righteous is futile.

While the Mosaic Law came by Moses, grace and truth came by Jesus Christ. Grace and truth are synonymous; you can't have one without the other (John 1:14-17). Many Christians don't understand the relationship between law and grace, and they think that Jesus actually came to give more law. In the four Gospels (which are actually pre-New Testament because Jesus had not yet died), He elevated the law solely for the purpose of teaching the Jews, all of whom followed the law at that time. Because of this, many believers misunderstand Jesus' purpose in referencing the law in so many of His teachings. They take this to mean that Jesus was all about Christians following rules and guidelines to please God. When Jesus referenced the law, He was actually pointing out that righteousness can't be obtained through self-effort. By highlighting how difficult the law was to keep, He pointed us to our need for a Savior. He was bringing a new paradigm, a kingdom paradigm that was based on grace, to the earth.

Jesus was a Jew who was subject to the regulations of Mosaic Law. He kept the law perfectly so that He could redeem people from it through the payment of His blood. The law was given to be a "schoolmaster," to show us the need for a Savior; but in Christ, we are no longer under the law and its penalties (Galatians 3:23-29). For a Christian to try to keep the law today as a means of securing his or her righteousness is simply error.

## WHY WORKING FOR RIGHTEOUSNESS IS FUTILE

The power of the new covenant is that God takes us out of the equation. This is why working for righteousness is futile. Unfortunately, the belief that we can earn righteousness is common among many believers. However, it is a sign of spiritual immaturity. Spiritually mature people realize that righteousness is a free gift that cannot be earned. You are spiritually mature when you no longer rely on the law to tell you what to do and when you no longer look to rules and regulations to dictate your behavior. Spiritual sons and daughters trust in the grace of God and the Holy Spirit to personally teach, lead, and guide them through life. When the Holy Spirit is leading you, your life will always please God.

As a result of the ransom that was paid with Jesus' blood, our relationship with the law has changed (Romans 6:14). This is vital to understand if you are going to truly experience the liberty that comes from a personal relationship with Jesus. In Christ, you are dead to the law so that you can be married to Jesus and be personally led by Him (Romans 7:4-6). Galatians 2:19, *AMPC*, says, "*For I through the Law [under the operation of the curse of the Law] have [in Christ's death for me] myself died to the Law and all the Law's demands upon me, so that I may [henceforth] live to and for God.*" When placed against the grace of God, the law falls incredibly short. While it was given to us to point us to our need for Jesus, the law is not the source of our righteousness and was never intended to be. Our righteousness is now based in Christ; therefore, Christ is the end of the law for believers (Romans 10:4)! If you are led by the Spirit, you are not under the law (Galatians 5:18).

## THROWING AWAY THE LAW?

Sometimes, in the conversation about grace, the idea that the law is irrelevant gets thrown around. Let's be clear—the law served a purpose, and it still does. Jesus came to fulfill the law, not throw it away (Matthew 5:17). The thing is that the law just doesn't have anything to do with the new-covenant Christian. The law was not made for righteous people, but for sinners (1 Timothy 1:9). It was instituted to provide clear guidelines for unrighteous people who didn't have the Holy Spirit living in them and didn't have the capacity to be led by God from their spirits. Anyone who does not have the Holy Spirit living in them needs exterior guidelines to help them stay on track. But once a person receives Jesus Christ as Lord and Savior, he or she has the internal compass of the Holy Spirit. This internal "GPS" provides the necessary navigation in life to help them make good decisions. Even when bad decisions are made, and there are consequences for those decisions, the Holy Spirit is there to re-route them so they can reach their ultimate destination.

The law was designed to help people recognize that they had a sin problem, and it accomplished its purpose perfectly (1 Corinthians 15:56). With the law comes a revelation of sin and the knowledge of the transgression of sin. Before the law was instituted, people had no knowledge that what they were doing was wrong! For example, even though Abraham lied by trying to pass Sarah off as his sister to Pharaoh, he was not considered a liar because there was no law prohibiting lying. While it was sin, he wasn't held accountable for it because there was no law against it.

Similarly, Adam didn't realize that his actions were inherently sinful. He knew what God had told him, but he didn't know it was "sin" as we know now. God had to implement the law because people had no concept of right and wrong. They were living ungodly lives but thought they were okay.

But even before the law was put into place, God's grace was in operation. For example, God made a promise to Abraham, even though he was a sinner. Genesis 12:1-4 says:

> Now the Lord had said unto Abram, Get thee out of thy country, and from thy kindred, and from thy father's house, unto a land that I will shew thee: And I will make of thee a great nation, and I will bless thee, and make thy name great; and thou shalt be a blessing: And I will bless them that bless thee, and curse him that curseth thee: and in thee shall all families of the earth be blessed. So Abram departed, as the Lord had spoken unto him; and Lot went with him: and Abram was seventy and five years old when he departed out of Haran.

Abraham did not have a born-again spirit, yet God extended grace to him. How much more is grace available then to those who are in Christ? According to the Bible,

Abraham's lies didn't stop God's favor from being extended to him, and the strife between Abraham and Lot didn't stop His favor either (Genesis 13:7). God delivered Abraham's enemies into his hands despite Abraham's flaws and shortcomings (Genesis 14:20). What did Abraham do to deserve God showing up and talking to him? Why did God consider him righteous, even though he hadn't actually done anything to deserve it? *"And he believed in the Lord; and he counted it to him for righteousness"* (Genesis 15:6). Abraham simply believed, and that is all we have to do to receive the benefits of the new covenant. God's covenant with us is one of faithfulness, mercy, and love that is completely based on *His* faithfulness to us, not our faithfulness to Him.

A powerful picture of our relationship with God under the new covenant versus under the law can be found in the example of Abraham's two sons. One, Isaac, was born from God's prophetic promise and one, Ishmael, was born out of self-effort. God promised Abraham that he would be the father of many nations, and that promise would come to pass through a son. But through impatience and doubt, Abraham and Sarah took matters into their own hands and attempted to bring the promise to pass in their own ability. Abraham had sex with Sarah's maid, Hagar, and she became pregnant with a son. However, this was not the son through which the promise of God would come. That pregnancy was the result of self-effort, not the supernatural power of God.

So, what does this story have to do with us today? As new-covenant people, we are children of the supernatural. We came into the family of God through faith in Him, alone, not our own works or efforts, just like Isaac came to Abraham and Sarah through faith. When you are born of grace and not the law, you bypass natural processes and move into the supernatural realm. When you operate in the supernatural, you receive supernatural favor. Understanding the covenant of grace gives you a proper perspective of the law. You can see that its purpose is to show you the need for saving grace through Christ. It is perfect in that it fulfills its objective. We don't discard the law. It serves a valuable purpose, and we can learn from it; but we don't use it as a measuring stick by which to live our lives under the new covenant. We have something far more powerful than the law at work in our lives, and it is the grace of God.

## NOTHING MORE TO ADD

There is always a tendency to want to add more to what God has said or done, but there is no need to do so. Man's works cannot be added to the finished works of Christ. You cannot gain access to God's favor through self-effort, nor can you benefit from the supernatural covenant of grace when you possess a law-based mindset. God does not remember our sins once we receive Jesus, and He promises to teach us to know Him through a personal, intimate relationship with the Holy Spirit. This relationship is not based on rules or regulations, but moment-by-moment guidance. This is how God wants us to live.

The beauty of the new covenant is that God remains faithful to us even when we are not faithful to Him. Second Timothy 2:13 says, *"If we believe not, yet he abideth faithful: he cannot deny himself."* We must believe and have faith in God's faithfulness to us. In fact, failure to believe this simple truth hinders what God can really do in our lives. When we don't rest in the finished works of Jesus, we inevitably fall back into performance and self-effort. These lead to condemnation and a sense of failure when we don't measure up. The covenant of grace is about the fact that we don't deserve His grace, but God loves us so much that He extended it to us through His Son. Jesus drew all judgment to Himself on the cross (John 12:32). We receive the benefits of God's grace by faith. By doing so, we allow the finished works of Christ to manifest in and through our lives.

# STUDY QUESTIONS

1. The law came by Moses, but ______________________ and __________________ came by Jesus Christ.

2. In the Gospels, Jesus elevated the law for the purpose of:
   A. showing Christians how to live successful lives.
   B. demonstrating humanity's need for a Savior.
   C. emphasizing the importance of adhering to God's guidelines.

3. True or False: Working for righteousness is a sign of spiritual immaturity.

4. For whom was the law given? ____________________________________________
_______________________________________________________________________
_______________________________________________________________________
_______________________________________________________________________

5. True or False: The grace of God was in operation before the law was established.

6. God counted Abraham as righteous because:
   A. he believed.
   B. he did righteous things.
   C. he was special to God.

7. You can't benefit from the supernatural covenant of grace when you possess a

    ____________________________________________.

8. True or False: As new-covenant believers, God no longer remembers our sins.

9. If you don't believe and rest in the finished works of Jesus, you will inevitably fall back into ____________________________________.

# ANSWER KEY

1. grace; truth
2. B
3. True
4. for sinners
5. True
6. A
7. law-based mindset
8. True
9. performance and self effort

**SCRIPTURE REFERENCES**

John 1:14-17
Galatians 4:4
Romans 11:11
Galatians 3:23-29
Romans 6:14
Romans 7:4-6
Galatians 2:19, *AMPC*
Romans 10:4
Galatians 5:18
Matthew 5:17
1 Timothy 1:9
1 Corinthians 15:56
Genesis 12:1-4, 12
Genesis 13:7
Genesis 14:20
Genesis 15:6
2 Timothy 2:13
John 12:32

# CHAPTER THIRTEEN
# A CHANGE OF PRIESTHOOD

Fully walking in the blessings of the new covenant requires an understanding of that covenant and the difference between the Law of Moses and the covenant of grace. The idea that the New Testament begins with the book of Matthew is actually incorrect. While it challenges religious thinking, the truth is that the death of Jesus is actually when the New Testament era began. Jesus' role when He came to this earth was two-fold: He came as a Jewish man operating under the dispensation of the law, while simultaneously prophesying about the new era of grace that was to come. The two ministries of Jesus must be clearly identified in the four Gospels; otherwise you will apply His law-based teachings in Matthew, Mark, Luke, and John to new-covenant realities, causing confusion and religious bondage. Rightly dividing the Word of God is essential to knowing how to operate under the covenant of grace.

One of the reasons so many Christians get into condemnation about their faults, flaws, and mistakes is because they don't understand the new covenant. They are limited because their views of God's character are based on how He dealt with people under the law. However, there are four key components of the new covenant that apply to us now that we are born again: first, the new covenant guarantees that Jesus will be our High Priest forever; second, He promises to never leave or forsake us; third, He is faithful to Himself and His Word above all else; and fourth, Jesus promises to be our guarantee of a better covenant (Hebrews 7:15-28; Hebrews 8:6). God swore by Himself these four things, which means that they are unalterable and eternal (Hebrews 6:16-20). That's good news!

Every human being has and always will fall grossly short of the mark when it comes to being faithful to God. Despite our best efforts, we simply cannot fulfill the requirements of the law. Knowing this, God implemented a new system that is based on His promise to be faithful to us, not on how well man could honor Him. This new covenant is about His commitment to be our God forever, no matter what (Hebrews 13:5). This isn't a license to do whatever we want; it is about allowing His faithfulness to give birth to such love for Him that we want to follow His will.

When we place our faithfulness to God in the spotlight, we minimize the premise of the new covenant and ignore the grace of God. Under the new covenant, even when we are unfaithful, God is faithful to us. There is nothing we can do that could nullify His commitment to us. Under this covenant of grace, God needs us to have faith in the faithfulness of Jesus. His faithfulness is not like man's faithfulness; **it will never fail!**

## A NEW COVENANT WITH NEW TERMS

Galatians 5:1 talks about the importance of standing free from the law and not returning to the bondage of self-effort and self-performance. God hasn't given the born-again Christian a bunch of rules and laws; He has given the Holy Spirit to lead and guide us, which requires a higher level of trust and dependence on Him. The Holy Spirit instructs us in ways that the law never could, which is why the covenant of grace is superior to the law (Galatians 5:13). For example, the law tells you not to commit adultery, but the Holy Spirit will show you how to treat your spouse on a daily basis, and avoid the situations that could lead to adultery in the first place. The law can't give that type of guidance.

So, let's look at how God's agreement with man changed under the new covenant. Under the law, God responded to man favorably or unfavorably based on what he did. God had a part and man had a part. If man didn't fulfill his end of the bargain, God wouldn't fulfill His part. If man disobeyed the law, he received a curse. If he obeyed the law, he received a blessing.

The new covenant operates in a completely different way. God does His part and man simply responds with belief and thanksgiving. In this new agreement between God and man, no curse results from disobedience to the law. Only blessings are available through the finished works of Christ. Jesus is the High Priest of the new covenant (Hebrews 4:14), and He forever intercedes for us before the Father (Hebrews 7:25). Unlike under the old covenant, you don't have to worry about God withdrawing His faithfulness to you if you miss the mark. There is no need to offer continual sacrifices for your sins. You are empowered to walk in holiness, righteousness, and truth because you are in Christ. This new covenant is about believing in what He did for you.

Not surprisingly, the covenant of grace was in effect long before the law was even established. Abraham is a great example. He received blessings and favor from God, such as reaping the spoils of victory in battle. God delivered Abraham from his enemies and enabled him to have success in the things he did. God even spoke that he would be the father of many nations and Abraham was not a believer. This was the grace of God in operation in Abraham's life.

When Abraham experienced victory in battle, he brought a tithe of the spoils to the high priest, Melchizedek, and the first word out of the priest's mouth was, "Blessed." What was Abraham's only response? "Thank you." Before there was any law on tithing, Abraham brought his tithe to the high priest as an act of appreciation (Genesis 14:17-20). This is an example of what it means to tithe under grace. Anything done under the law brings fear and bondage; but tithing under grace brings liberty. The covenant of grace is all about acting out of love for God, not religious compulsion or fear. When you truly know what Jesus secured for you through His sacrifice, your actions are a form of worship to Him.

## GETTING RID OF SIN-CONSCIOUSNESS

There are several references to "perfection" in the New Testament (Hebrews 7:11; Hebrews 9:9). Sometimes Christians think this means they are to maintain a standard of perfection so as not to suffer the wrath of God. However, these references to perfection actually mean having a consciousness that isn't scarred by the effects of sin. A mind that is free from condemnation and guilt is a mind that is infused with the truth of what Jesus has done. By continually meditating on the power of the blood of Jesus, you can maintain a righteousness-consciousness, even when you miss the mark.

So, what is sin-consciousness? It is a state of mind that is marked by a perpetual awareness of sin. When you have a seared conscience, you are not responding to what the blood of Jesus has done for you (1 Timothy 4:2). It brings condemnation, guilt, and shame. Teaching people to live holy lives doesn't help them to live holy. Christianity is about trusting God to make you holy, not in rules and laws. Rules and laws can't keep you free from condemnation. In fact, they exacerbate the guilt and shame that come from sin. This is where the Holy Spirit comes in. His job is to convince you not to be sin-conscious, but to be righteousness-conscious (John 16:8). The conscience is the voice that tells us when we do wrong; but a perfect conscience allows you to acknowledge and accept what the blood of Jesus has done for you, without reservation.

Being consumed with your mistakes keeps you from your freedom in Christ and from having your consciousness perfected by grace. You can't carry out the wonderful things God has for you to do because you feel so terrible about your past. However, when your heart doesn't condemn you, you have confidence in God, which is critical to receiving from Him (1 John 3:21). The beauty of the grace of God is that it sets people free from an evil conscience and allows their faith to work properly.

Please understand that curses will never come from Jesus toward His people under the new covenant of grace. Sin is under the curse, which entered the earth when Adam disobeyed God in the garden of Eden. So when you miss the mark and continue in that flow, you put *yourself* in the flow of the curse. That is not God's doing. God is only concerned with blessing you. That is why He wants us to receive Jesus' finished works. The fact that there was a need for a second covenant lets us know that the first one was not flawless (Hebrews 8:6-8). This new covenant is absolutely fail-proof because it is completely dependent on Him and His faithfulness, not our works (2 Corinthians 3:1-18). Because He cannot lie or fail, we can rest in the surety of the covenant of grace. The only way you can fail in this new covenant is to not believe it. Spiritual warfare is maintaining the stance of victory that has been secured for you by Jesus.

## RECONCILING THE HARSH TEACHINGS OF JESUS WITH NEW COVENANT REALITIES

A lack of understanding about Jesus' harsh teachings in the Gospels has brought much bondage to the body of Christ. Things like the instruction to cut off your hand if it causes you to sin (Mark 9:43), forgive others or God won't forgive you (Matthew 6:14, 15), be perfect just like God (Matthew 5:48), sell everything you have (Matthew 19:21), and pluck out your eye if you lust after someone (Mark 9:47) have been taught as New-Testament instructions, and brought fear and sin-consciousness. But, what was Jesus really saying in these examples? Brilliantly, He was making it impossible for anyone to comply with these rules, thus demonstrating that there was no way people could keep the law in their own ability (Matthew 5:20). He was paving the way for a higher way of life: grace through a relationship with Him.

Through these harsh Gospel teachings, Jesus established Himself as the grace "bridge" between the old and new covenants. He revealed the true spirit behind the law, and He prophesied about the new covenant that was to come. He gave people a glimpse of the new paradigm He was bringing to the earth. Because He was a Jewish man born under the law (Galatians 4:4, 5) and His audience at the time was under the law as well, He was perfectly equipped to lay the groundwork for the new kingdom reality that was on the horizon.

When we try to take something that Jesus taught under the law and apply it to the dispensation of grace, it causes problems because new-covenant people are no longer under the law. The new covenant actually began after Jesus died. It was His death, not birth, that brought in the new covenant and the New Testament era (Hebrews 9:17). Realizing Jesus' true intent with His teachings in the four Gospels helps people feel the freedom of grace as we live on this side of the cross.

No human being has ever successfully practiced the law without fail. Through the law, we encounter failure, not success. It stirs up sin, then pushes us further into condemnation. Jesus showed us that practicing the law perfectly was an impossibility and that no human being could approach the level of righteousness that He required through their own efforts or works. This is the beauty of grace. It allows us to receive God's righteousness by faith in Jesus, and takes the pressure off of us to perform and attain favor from God on our own merit. There is no better news than this!

# STUDY QUESTIONS

1. True or False: The New Testament begins with the Gospels.

2. What are the four premises of the new covenant? ______________________________

3. The law was predicated on ______________________________.

4. How have the terms of the new covenant changed compared to the old covenant?

5. True or False: The covenant of grace was operating before the law was established.

6. When the Word talks about "perfection" in Hebrews 7:11 and Hebrews 9:9, to what is it referring? ______________________________________________

______________________________________________

______________________________________________

______________________________________________

7. Sin-consciousness is ______________________________________________

______________________________________________.

8. What is the Holy Spirit's job? ______________________________________________

______________________________________________

______________________________________________

______________________________________________

9. The new covenant is completely dependent on God and His ____________________

______________________________________________.

10. What was Jesus trying to communicate through His harsh Gospel teachings? _____

______________________________________________

______________________________________________

______________________________________________

# ANSWER KEY

1. False
2. Jesus would be our priest forever; He would never leave or forsake us; He would be faithful to Himself and His Word; He would be our guarantee of a better covenant.
3. man having a part and God having a part. If man didn't fulfill his end of the bargain, God wouldn't fulfill His part.
4. Under the new covenant, God has a part and man simply responds with belief and thanksgiving. There is no curse, only blessing. Jesus is the High Priest of the new covenant and He forever intercedes for us before the Father.
5. True
6. It is referring to not having sin-consciousness.
7. a consciousness that is marked by a perpetual awareness of sin
8. to convince us of our righteousness
9. faithfulness
10. He was making it impossible for anyone to comply with His teaching, thus demonstrating that there was no way they could actually keep the law in their own ability.

**SCRIPTURE REFERENCES**

Hebrews 7:15-28

Hebrews 8:6-8

Hebrews 6:16-20

Hebrews 13:5

Galatians 5:1

Galatians 5:13

Hebrews 4:14

Genesis 14:17-20

Hebrews 7:11

Hebrews 9:9

1 Timothy 4:2

John 16:8

1 John 3:21

2 Corinthians 3:1-18

Mark 9:43

Matthew 6:14, 15

Matthew 5:48

Matthew 19:21

Mark 9:47

Matthew 5:20

Galatians 4:4, 5

Hebrews 9:17

# CHAPTER FOURTEEN
# GRACE FOR LIFE

The grace of God is more than just something Christians say to sound spiritual, it is the centerpiece of Jesus' whole message. With it being such an important aspect of the Christian life, it is vital that we understand all that we can about it so that we can benefit from it in our walk with God. Grace is the power behind everything that God does and it is what gives us access to eternal life and a life of abundance while we are on the earth. The shedding of Jesus' blood was an act of grace that enabled all people who receive Him to experience the benefits of His finished works. As a spiritual force, grace is multifaceted and actually has three active components: saving grace, standing grace, and serving grace. Exploring each type of grace will solidify the purpose of grace in our lives and teach us how it works to help us live godly lives.

First, let's look at John 1:14, 17, "*And the Word was made flesh, and dwelt among us, (and we beheld his glory, the glory as of the only begotten of the Father,) full of grace and truth...For the law was given by Moses, but grace and truth came by Jesus Christ.*" These Scriptures show us a few things. First, it says that Jesus was full of grace and truth. If Jesus was full of grace and truth, grace is more than a simple Bible subject.

Jesus is actually the expression of God's grace, the fullness of it personified. Through Him we are empowered to overcome the world, the flesh, and the devil. Believing and receiving this truth is the key.

The grace of God is not just for salvation, but also for transformation. It is given to work through us and touch someone else's life in order to be a blessing to them. The moment you received Jesus as your Lord and personal Savior, grace moved on your heart and you were instantly translated out of the kingdom of darkness and into the kingdom of God. Your spirit was recreated in a split second and you were born again. The same grace that saved you in that moment is also responsible for your walk with God going from glory to glory and your mind being renewed. The more you exercise your faith in the power of God's grace operating in your life, and the more you behold Jesus by letting the Word of God be the mirror that reflects back to you who you really are, the more you allow grace to transform you into His image. Grace is the catalyst for great change in a person's life, which is why you can then make a difference in the lives of others. It is all because of His grace.

The different types of grace have different functions. Saving grace is God working for us, doing things we cannot do on our own. Standing grace is God working *in* us, to help us improve ourselves and resist the temptation that leads to sin. Finally, serving grace is how God works through us, using us to bless other people.

The whole foundation of Christianity is the belief and understanding that we cannot save ourselves in any form or fashion. The idea that man can somehow achieve salvation through good works is embraced by different religions and belief systems. Somehow, as human beings, we think that we have what it takes to earn our salvation. We equate good works with being a good person and believe that God likes good people more than those who are "bad" by our standards. The truth is that, without Jesus, none of us stand a chance. This is why saving grace is necessary for eternal life. No other religion can provide what Jesus provides: salvation based on the grace of God, and not human effort (Ephesians 2:1-9). No other human being that ever lived can secure our right-standing with God besides Him. We simply cannot save ourselves! This is the core belief that has to be in place in order to receive salvation.

Ephesians 2:8, 9 says, "*For by grace are ye saved through faith; and that not of yourselves: it is the gift of God: Not of works, lest any man should boast.*" Here we see why God set the system up to be totally dependent on Him. He eliminated any tendency we may have to take any credit for our salvation. God, alone, wants to get the glory for the redemption of mankind. He wants to be in the midst of everything good that affects us. Not only does it remove the pride attached to accomplishment through self-effort, salvation through grace takes the pressure off of us to try to earn God's love and approval (Romans 1:16).

The grace of God, like anything else that comes from Him, is manifested by faith. We are delivered from judgment through free grace, not through our own striving. Grace is manifested by faith; therefore, we are saved by grace. This makes us partakers of a multitude of benefits and blessings that we do not deserve. We are not justified or made righteous by the law; it is only our faith in Jesus Christ that is able to save us (Galatians 2:16). We have access to everything that Jesus' blood purchased for us.

## THE DIFFERENCE BETWEEN GRACE AND FAITH

While grace and faith work in tandem, it is important to note that they are not the same thing. Faith is a *product* of grace. Three days after Jesus died on the cross, He appeared publicly, very much alive and well. His death and resurrection were both acts of grace. His appearance to His disciples afterward gave birth to their faith in His redemptive work. Once grace did its job, faith came forth.

Similarly, the apostle Paul preached the Gospel of Grace. Acts 14:9, 10 says, "*The same heard Paul speak: who stedfastly beholding him, and perceiving that he had faith to be healed, Said with a loud voice, Stand upright on thy feet. And he leaped and walked.*" The grace of God preached leads to faith, which results in healing and deliverance. It is by grace that we are healed, delivered, and made to prosper. Faith is the product of grace, which is why it is so important that the Gospel of Grace is preached. Signs and wonders will always follow.

When it comes to receiving from God, the foundation of the message of grace is always the understanding that we can never qualify for His blessings, no matter how hard we try. We must have faith in God and the blessings He has promised us, not in our qualification for those blessings. The thought that we can lay hold of God's blessings without grace can leave us discouraged, and rightfully so. Human effort will never be enough to bring us into the realm of God and what belongs to Him.

When it comes to favor and blessings, Jesus is all about equal opportunity! He does not discriminate, but will bless anyone and everyone who trusts and believes in Him. Matthew 9:28, 29 is a great example of this. It says, "*And when he was come into the house, the blind men came to him: and Jesus saith unto them, Believe ye that I am able to do this? They said unto him, Yea, Lord. Then touched he their eyes, saying, According to your faith be it unto you.*" When the blind men came to Jesus for healing, He first established their belief in Him. This is the criteria for any type of creative miracle. After their faith was confirmed, their healing was manifested.

The woman with the issue of blood is another example of how faith lays hold of Jesus' healing and delivering power:

> And a certain woman, which had an issue of blood twelve years, And had suffered many things of many physicians, and had spent all that she had, and was nothing bettered, but rather grew worse, When she had heard of Jesus, came in the press behind, and touched his garment. For she said, If I may touch but his clothes, I shall be whole. And straightway the fountain of her blood was dried up; and she felt in her body that she was healed of that plague. And Jesus, immediately knowing in himself that virtue had gone out of him, turned him about in the press, and said, Who touched my clothes? And his disciples said unto him, Thou seest the multitude thronging thee, and sayest thou, Who touched me? And he looked round about to see her that had done this thing. But the woman fearing and trembling, knowing what was done in her, came and fell down before him, and told him all the truth. And he said unto her, Daughter, thy faith hath made thee whole; go in peace, and be whole of thy plague (Mark 5:25-34).

Jesus was the grace of God personified and this woman's faith in Jesus (grace) made her whole.

We did not deserve God's love, but He chose to love us anyway by sending His only Son to die for us (Romans 5:8). As unworthy as we were, Jesus revived us from spiritual death to life. Even when we are on our worst behavior, He still shows us His best. The power of God's love is that it does not require us to do anything in order to access it. It simply loves without conditions or stipulations (Romans 8:32). When you trust in grace, who is Jesus, you will experience His goodness, and the faith for the miraculous will be released. When grace flows into every aspect of your life, it will save you, help you stand in the truth that empowers you to live a godly life, and enable you to serve and love others unconditionally.

# STUDY QUESTIONS

1. True or False: Jesus is grace personified.

2. Grace helps us to resist ______________________________.

3. The grace of God is not just for salvation but for ____________________.

4. The three types of grace are ______________________________

   ______________________________

   ______________________________.

5. The foundation of Christianity is the belief that:

   A. our good works can help us achieve righteousness.

   B. God is angry with those who sin.

   C. we cannot achieve salvation on our own.

6. True or False: No other religion can lead to salvation.

7. Why is salvation through grace a better way? ____________________

   ______________________________

   ______________________________

   ______________________________

8. True or False: Faith is born out of grace.

9. What is the foundational message of grace? ______________________

______________________________________________

______________________________________________

______________________________________________

10. The criteria for any type of creative miracle is:

    A. faith.

    B. being a good person.

    C. having an issue that God deems worthy of fixing.

# ANSWER KEY

1. True
2. sin
3. transformation
4. saving grace, standing grace, and serving grace
5. C
6. True
7. because it takes the pressure off of us to have to achieve salvation through our own efforts
8. True
9. we can never qualify for His blessings
10. A

**SCRIPTURE REFERENCES**

John 1:14, 17

Ephesians 2:1-9

Romans 1:16

Galatians 2:16

Acts 14:9, 10

Matthew 9:28, 29

Mark 5:25-34

Romans 5:8

Romans 8:32

# CHAPTER FIFTEEN
# THE PURPOSE OF GRACE

When you know the purpose for something you are able to utilize it to its fullest capacity. This is true in dealing with both spiritual and natural things. Jesus is the grace of God personified and, through Him, we are empowered to do and have things that we can't do or have through our own ability. Grace is the power of God unto salvation (Romans 1:16). It is His ability working in and through us to save us, stand in the face of sin and overcome it, and serve others. Jesus is constantly working in us and making us victorious. The grace of God that is responsible for our salvation is what changes us from the inside out and purifies us on a daily basis, enabling us to stand before God without guilt, shame, or condemnation. It empowers us in every area of our lives, yet makes us humble. Grace is the unmerited, undeserved favor of God and it is operating in the life of every person who has accepted Jesus as Lord and Savior.

We have established that there are three different types of grace. There is the grace that saves us, the grace that helps us to stand, and the grace that enables us to serve others. In addition, God's grace delivers us from evil and redeems our lives from all kinds of destruction. Jude 1:24, 25, *AMPC*, says:

> Now to Him Who is able to keep you without stumbling or slipping or falling, and to present [you] unblemished (blameless and faultless) before the presence of His glory in triumphant joy and exultation [with unspeakable, ecstatic delight]—To the one only God, our Savior through Jesus Christ our Lord, be glory (splendor), majesty, might and dominion, and power and authority, before all time and now and forever (unto all the ages of eternity). Amen (so be it).

Jesus, through His grace, can keep us from falling, present us faultless before the throne of God, and enable us to enter into His presence with joy!

Grace works in us to help us not only endure trials and tribulations, but overcome difficult circumstances as well. When we receive the grace of God for our lives, we are releasing Jesus, Himself, into our situations. Second Corinthians 12:9, 10 says, "*And he said unto me, My grace is sufficient for thee: for my strength is made perfect in weakness. Most gladly therefore will I rather glory in my infirmities, that the power of Christ may rest upon me. Therefore I take pleasure in infirmities, in reproaches, in necessities, in persecutions, in distresses for Christ's sake: for when I am weak, then am I strong.*" The apostle Paul knew all too well the pain of hardship, but he relied on God's grace to bring him through. We have the same access to the grace of God to bring us through our trials and tribulations.

God's grace is immeasurable and unlimited. No matter what the level of the challenging circumstance is, the grace of God will always come to you in a measure that is above the circumstance. No matter what situation we find ourselves in, His grace is greater than all our sins. In Second Corinthians 12:7, Paul mentions a "thorn in the flesh." This wasn't referencing a sickness or disease, but rather something that Paul was dealing with personally that was a continual reminder to him of his need for God's grace. He prayed for God to remove it but the Lord didn't remove this thorn. It was something that caused him to press into God further and allow God's grace to strengthen Him in the midst of the trial. Paul was empowered to endure through faith that was born out of the grace of God working in his life and ministry.

We will also face situations that require us to rely on the grace of God, even though we would just prefer that He remove the challenge. While there are times when God will do so, there are times when He won't. Instead, He requires us to lean on Him so that, in our weakness, His strength is made perfect through His grace.

Grace also calls for us to possess the right attitude. Jesus and the apostle Paul are wonderful examples of enduring through difficulties with an attitude of humility. When Jesus began the process of taking on the weight of the world's sin in the garden of Gethsemane, He asked for God to take the cup from Him, referring to the suffering that He was about to endure (Matthew 26:36-46). He immediately tapped into the grace of God when He deferred to the Father's will being done instead of His own. Even while He was being crucified, He asked the Father to forgive murderers (Luke 23:34). He did not cry out once to complain or murmur against God in the midst of excruciating pain. He powered through the crucifixion by the grace of God. It was grace that enabled Him to complete His assignment.

In life, we will face many different situations that will challenge our faith and require us to rely on God's grace to carry us through. The death of a loved one, divorce or separation, the loss of a job, and a host of other tough situations will force us to lean on God's ability instead of our own. In fact, our ability could never hold up in the face of the things that life throws at us. It is during those times that we can put our words to work, declaring that there is a specific grace to get through whatever the situation may be. When we do this, it will produce faith in God's strength to get through. This faith will keep us focused on Him as we walk through the trial or difficulty. Grace is the catalyst for victory, no matter what is going on around us or in our lives.

Humility is a key to receiving the grace necessary to overcome whatever we face. First Peter 5:5-8 says:

> Likewise, ye younger, submit yourselves unto the elder. Yea, all of you be subject one to another, and be clothed with humility: for God resisteth the proud, and giveth grace to the humble. Humble yourselves therefore under the mighty hand of God, that he may exalt you in due time: Casting all your care upon him; for he careth for you. Be sober, be vigilant; because your adversary the devil, as a roaring lion, walketh about, seeking whom he may devour.

When we humble ourselves by submitting to God's will and letting Him have all our cares, Satan cannot devour us. When we rest in the Lord, we allow His grace to work on our behalf.

What are you facing that requires you to cast your cares over on the Lord? Is it a financial or relationship issue? Maybe you are going through a really difficult time that you have no idea how you will manage to overcome. No matter what it is, when you put your faith in the grace of God that is working on your behalf, you will find a supernatural strength and ability to endure the situation. Knowing that you are powerless to fix whatever the situation is will put you in a perfect position to fully rely on God and His grace. It is a wonderful feeling to know that you do not have to face these things alone or in your own strength.

Standing grace is the kind of grace that empowers us to remain strong in the face of temptation and sin. Grace helps us say yes to Jesus and no to the enticements of the devil. Each of us will be faced with situations that are designed to lure us into compromise, but knowing God has not left you to fight those battles in your own strength is a major sense of relief. Many Christians don't realize the power that is at their disposal, and so they feel that they have to give in to temptation. This is simply not true. Part of the salvation package includes the power to overcome sin. We possess the grace to overcome sin because He lives in us.

So many believers give up on turning away from ungodliness because they lose sight of what they possess. Titus 2:11, 12 says, "*For the grace of God that bringeth salvation hath appeared to all men, Teaching us that, denying ungodliness and worldly lusts, we should live soberly, righteously, and godly, in this present world.*" Grace teaches us to deny ungodliness and live in a way that pleases God. How can you put this into practical use? Allow the grace of God to strengthen you every moment of the day and consciously lean into that grace when you are faced with choices. It is about relying on grace to empower you when you feel weak by turning your thoughts and intentions toward it. The next time you are faced with a situation in which you know the enemy is trying to lure you into a sin trap, take a moment and pause. Declare inwardly, remind yourself that you possess the grace necessary to overcome, and then lean into that ability in that moment (Romans 6:14). You will be amazed at the faith that rises up in you to remove yourself from the situation or avoid it in some other way that God shows you.

The beauty of grace is that God offers it to us while we are still sinners. He doesn't wait until we are perfect and all is right in our world before we can benefit from grace. We need grace in order to have the faith for salvation! Every person has the ability to partake of the healing, wholeness, deliverance, and eternal life that Jesus secured for them. Through grace we can have dominion over the sin that once held us in bondage and much more. Trusting in the grace of God is the key.

Philippians 2:13, *AMPC*, says, *"[Not in your own strength] for it is God Who is all the while effectually at work in you [energizing and creating in you the power and desire], both to will and to work for His good pleasure and satisfaction and delight."* God is committed to work in us and He will create in us the desire to do His will. Jesus is Grace, and the Word instructs us to come to the throne of grace so that we can obtain mercy and help in our time of need (Hebrews 4:16). Mercy spares us from getting the bad things we deserve when we miss the mark, and grace bestows on us the good things we do not deserve. It strengthens us to overcome temptation and empowers us to live a godly life. Jesus is the grace of God who works in and through our lives to bring us to a place of abundant living on the earth. Simply believe and receive what He has done!

# STUDY QUESTIONS

1. True or False: Grace can deliver us from any and all situations.

2. What are three things that grace can do for us? ______________________

   ______________________

   ______________________

   ______________________

3. When we turn our ______________________

   over to God, He turns them into ______________________.

4. True or False: As Christians, we are called to suffer.

5. How do we humble ourselves?

   A. by praying more

   B. by submitting to God's will

   C. by giving to the poor

6. God's grace is allowed to work in our lives when we ______________________

   ______________________.

7. Grace empowers us to:

   A. say no to sin.

   B. live righteously.

   C. both A and B.

8. True or False: Grace has made salvation available to everyone.

9. Why is trusting in our willpower futile? ______________________________

   ______________________________________________________________

   ______________________________________________________________

   ______________________________________________________________

10. Mercy spares us from ______________________________________

    and grace bestows on us ___________________________________.

# ANSWER KEY

1. True
2. keep us from stumbling, present us faultless before God, allow us to go into His presence with unlimited joy and delight
3. weaknesses; strengths
4. False
5. B
6. rest in the Lord
7. C
8. True
9. because we cannot achieve victory over sin in our own ability
10. getting the bad things we deserve; the good things we do not deserve

**SCRIPTURE REFERENCES**

Romans 1:16
Jude 1:24, 25, *AMPC*
2 Corinthians 12:7, 9, 10
Matthew 26:36-46
Luke 23:34
1 Peter 5:5-8
Titus 2:11, 12
Romans 6:14
Philippians 2:13, *AMPC*
Hebrews 4:16

# CHAPTER SIXTEEN
# LIVING THE GRACE LIFE

Living the grace life is the high calling of every believer because it is a way of life that requires humility. It takes humility to relinquish self-effort and thinking that you can play a part in God blessing you. The new covenant was established and designed to be reliant on the finished works of Jesus. Grace helps us live an abundantly blessed life, and empowers us to do things that we cannot do on our own. Why would you want to live any other way? There is liberty in knowing that God has provided a way for us to live that frees us from self-effort and performance-based activities to secure righteousness or blessings. Making grace available to us is an act of the Father's love. God calls us according to His grace, and since grace is Jesus personified, it is actually Jesus calling us to a higher way of life.

First Timothy 1:12-14, 16 gives us some powerful insight into this grace life:

> And I thank Christ Jesus our Lord, who hath enabled me, for that he counted me faithful, putting me into the ministry; Who was before a blasphemer, and a persecutor, and injurious: but I obtained mercy, because I did it ignorantly in unbelief. And the grace of our Lord was exceeding abundant with faith and love

which is in Christ Jesus...Howbeit for this cause I obtained mercy, that in me first Jesus Christ might show forth all longsuffering, for a pattern to them which should hereafter believe on him to life everlasting.

Each person has been called to a specific assignment in life, and whatever talents and gifts we have are from God (2 Timothy 1:9, *AMPC*). It doesn't matter what mistakes we have made in the past or whether we have sinned, the call of God on our lives is irrevocable (Romans 11:29). God shows mercy to us because of His grace and is continually giving us opportunities to press into what He has for us.

Before the foundations of the world, we were called according to His grace, not our own works. When you know you are called and you know that everything you have been tasked to do by God will only happen through His ability, it frees you to tap into His great grace. God calls us out of the kingdom of darkness and delivers us from our sins. This is a holy calling to the vocation He has chosen for us. In submitting our gifts to Him and allowing Him to use them for His glory, we truly fulfill our purpose.

God's grace is also an identity-shaper; it makes us who we are. First Corinthians 15:10, *AMPC*, says, *"But by the grace (unmerited favor and blessing) of God I am what I am, and His grace toward me was not [found to be] for nothing (fruitless and without effect). In fact, I worked harder than all of them [the apostles], though it was not really I, but the grace (the unmerited favor and blessing) of God which was with me."* Because of God's grace, we accomplish more with less effort than others in the world who labor through their own efforts for their own glory. We are who and what we are through accepting the unmerited favor and blessing of God. His grace is what is responsible for your calling coming to fruition. Through His ability you can do great exploits and truly make a difference in this world. By surrendering to the grace of God that is on your life, your calling will be the light that draws others into His kingdom.

## SERVING GRACE: AN EMPOWERMENT FROM GOD

The grace that empowers is the grace that is to be utilized to serve others with your gift and through your life. When the Word says this grace is contained in earthen vessels, it is referring to each and every human being who is in Christ (2 Corinthians

4:7, *AMPC*). We are those vessels, carrying our gift and calling to the world. The grace did not originate with us, but came from God, Himself. We can choose to share it with others in order to be a blessing to them.

If you are uncertain whether or not there is a calling on *your* life, look at First Peter 4:10, 11, *AMPC*:

> As each of you has received a gift (a particular spiritual talent, a gracious divine endowment), employ it for one another as [befits] good trustees of God's many-sided grace [faithful stewards of the extremely diverse powers and gifts granted to Christians by unmerited favor]. Whoever speaks, [let him do it as one who utters] oracles of God; whoever renders service, [let him do it] as with the strength which God furnishes abundantly, so that in all things God may be glorified through Jesus Christ (the Messiah). To Him be the glory and dominion forever and ever (through endless ages). Amen (so be it).

Peter is letting us know that every person has received a special gift, talent, and ability that is to be used for the glory of God. These gifts are to be employed and shared with one another because, when we share them, we are acting as good stewards of His grace. Whatever we say, we should say it for the glory of God. Whatever we do, we should do for the glory of God. This translates to our jobs, businesses, and other things God has clearly called us to do. Whether it is in the church or outside the church, a believer has been graced to carry out a specific assignment for the Lord and possesses the spiritual equipment to do so.

When you discover your specific grace and what you've been called to do, there is a liberty that comes that enables you to now live life without toiling. In First Corinthians 15:10, the apostle Paul says, "*But by the grace of God I am what I am...*" He is acknowledging that everything about him and everything that he is doing and carrying out is only because of God's grace operating in and through his life. So likewise, the grace of God operating in and through your life is not supposed to be without effect. In other words, it is supposed to be bearing some fruit. It is supposed to impact the lives of people around you and in your world. We must be faithful stewards of this grace so that more lives can be brought into the kingdom of God.

The world does not understand the grace of God or the idea that self-effort cannot secure salvation. However, Jesus perfects us as we commit to walk with Him in spite of our flaws (Colossians 1:27-29). This is grace in action. As the ultimate servant, Jesus demonstrated how serving grace helps us reflect God in our interactions with people in a way that reverences Him (Hebrews 12:28). Throughout His ministry, He showed us what it means to serve others, and we are tasked with using our gifts, talents, and abilities to be conduits of His grace, pointing people back to Him (Philippians 2:12, 13, *AMPC*). He creates in us the desire to do His will and energizes us to get the job done. When we submit our gifts back to Him, He can use them to bring God glory and demonstrate what serving grace really looks like. Let's put our trust in God's grace and experience its reality and effect in every area of our lives.

# STUDY QUESTIONS

1. Living the grace life is the high calling of every believer because ________________ __________________________________________.

2. God's way of life frees us from:
   A. self-effort.
   B. responsibility.
   C. accountability.

3. True or False: Our gifts and talents were given to us for the purpose of glorifying God.

4. True or False: The call of God on a person's life can be removed if they sin.

5. How do we truly fulfill our purpose? ______________________________
______________________________________________
______________________________________________
______________________________________________

6. God's grace helps to shape our ______________________________.

7. True or False: Jesus perfects us in spite of our flaws.

# ANSWER KEY

1. it is a way of life that requires humility
2. A
3. True
4. False
5. by submitting our gifts to Him and allowing Him to use them for His glory
6. identity
7. True

**SCRIPTURE REFERENCES**

1 Timothy 1:12-14, 16

2 Timothy 1:9, *AMPC*

1 Corinthians 15:10, *AMPC*

2 Corinthians 4:7, *AMPC*

1 Peter 4:10, 11, *AMPC*

Colossians 1:27-29

Hebrews 12:28

Philippians 2:12, 13, *AMPC*

# CHAPTER SEVENTEEN
# THE CONSEQUENCES OF FALLING FROM GRACE

When you sit down in a chair, you don't question whether or not it can hold you. You trust and believe that when you sit down, you will be supported. The same thing is true when you walk into a room and turn a light switch on. There is no question, most of the time, that the light will come on when you flip that switch. These are examples of how unwavering trust applies to our everyday activities. It is unfortunate that we do not trust and rely on God the same way we do an inanimate object! To truly believe is to be totally dependent on someone or something. This is the way that we must trust God. If we are to depend on Jesus for our salvation, then it follows that we must depend on Him for everything else in our lives. Every part of the salvation package belongs to us, and we have to rely on His grace and truth if we want to enter into the rest that the Bible promises us (John 1:17).

The Ten Commandments Moses gave in the Old Testament focused on the many requirements the people had to fulfill to earn God's favor. The imperfect Law of Moses dictated that they work hard to keep the entire law in order to escape death, which meant that works replaced God's perfect grace. In fact, the law that came by Moses is referred to in the New Testament as the "ministration of death" (2 Corinthians 3:7). Under the law, it was about what man did first in order to get God to respond favorably. If man didn't abide by the instructions of the law, a curse would ensue. However, Jesus' resurrection changed that order around. We are no longer trying to fulfill a set of rules or laws in order to obtain God's blessing, but we rely on His unmerited favor and faithfulness to us.

Accepting God's grace requires a willingness to abandon our self-effort. This can be difficult to accept at first! Religion has trained us to hold on to the idea that we need to work for salvation, work for God's blessings, and be flawless in order to receive merciful treatment from Him. Religion teaches us that our behavior determines whether God favors us. Most believers believe that if they do good, then God will do good to them; if they do anything wrong, or sin, they will reap God's wrath, and certainly not receive His blessings. The idea of God's goodness and mercy being continually released toward His people in spite of their flaws is difficult to accept when you are holding on to a religious mindset. However, what Jesus did must be our sole confidence. What is recorded in the Scriptures is included so that we can believe in Him and have life through His name (John 20:30, 31).

Again, when you are used to religious teaching that emphasizes works and self-effort, it can be a challenge to embrace the benefits of the new covenant. However, we must depend on His grace if we want to live. The old covenant was based on self-effort; the Law of Moses was actually the ministry of death, written in stone. To try to abide by the mandates of the old covenant as new-covenant people is to fall from grace.

As human beings, we are always trying work our way to the top; it is part of our nature. Whether it is in our careers or personal goals, we live in a culture of self-effort. We are taught that if you don't make things happen for yourself, you will never get ahead. While it is true that there are things you need to do in this physical life to practically reach your goals, when it comes to spiritual realities, you do not have to work for God's approval or blessings. This is where "work" goes wrong. Our society is built upon the idea of self-reliance and this mindset, unfortunately, has translated to how we relate to God and His kingdom. However, when we try to secure favor from God through carnal means, it will only lead to frustration and anxiety. Not only that, we can't achieve righteousness or any other goal in the kingdom of God through our own efforts (Romans 11:6). This is religion. Yes, there is discipline involved in positioning ourselves for maximum effectiveness in the kingdom, but the promises of God have already been secured by Jesus with His death on the cross. We have access to an unlimited supply of God's blessing and provision through Jesus, alone, and it is by the grace of God that we can tangibly lay hold of these things.

If we look at the way the Israelites interacted with the old covenant in the book of Exodus, it becomes clear that their pride in thinking they could fulfill all the requirements of the law led to their downfall. When we take on this way of relating to God, we will also experience what is a true "fall from grace." Exodus 19:8 says, "*And all the people answered together, and said, All that the Lord hath spoken we will do. And Moses returned the words of the people unto the Lord.*" A casual reading of this Scripture may not reveal the issue, but the reason the Israelites' position was a problem was because it showed that they presumed to be able to keep every part of the law through their own efforts. However, the law was set up to point them to the need for a Savior, to show them that right-standing with God cannot be achieved through their efforts. If a person breaks even one commandment, he or she is guilty of breaking the entire law. The law was essentially given to prove to mankind that we need God.

God's plan to redeem mankind from the curse of the law was fulfilled through Jesus, but we often try to add to what has already been declared enough. We are to believe and depend on Jesus because His redemptive work has more than compensated for our shortcomings and sins. We can't make ourselves right in God's eyes and He doesn't want us to try. The Father sent Jesus to deliver us from having to live under the Law of Moses, from having to live under the curse of self-effort. Jesus didn't come to destroy the law, but to fulfill it. He assured the people that not one single word would be changed. "*Think not that I am come to destroy the law, or the prophets: I am not come to destroy, but to fulfil. For verily I say unto you, Till heaven and earth pass, one jot or one tittle shall in no wise pass from the law, till all be fulfilled*" (Matthew 5:17, 18).

The law strengthens sin, which is why Jesus came to redeem everyone living under it (1 Corinthians 15:56). He did this so we could be adopted as children of God (Galatians 4:4, 5). The reason that we cannot live under the law anymore is because it constantly reminds us of our sin. It is counterproductive to righteousness. No one can possibly be justified by the deeds of the law because the knowledge of the law brings the knowledge of sin (Romans 3:20). We've been redeemed from sin and the curse of the law through what Jesus has done for us.

### GOD'S UNMERITED FAVOR AT WORK

There are three definitions of grace that can give understanding of exactly what it is. First, grace is God's unmerited and undeserved favor. Second, it is God's infinite love and kindness toward man. Third, it is God's abounding, increasing provision of love for those who depend on Him. Religion pushes the idea that we have to try to do something that has already been done, but this is the opposite of how God wants us to operate. When it comes to God's grace and avoiding the consequences of falling from grace, it is vital to understand that Jesus, Himself, is God's unmerited, undeserved, unearned favor in human form. He is the Grace of God. Titus 2:11 says that the grace of God that brings salvation has appeared to all men. When there is no other choice but Jesus, He won't let you down. Grace teaches you how to deny ungodliness and live a holy life (Titus 2:12). When you have no other option except Jesus as your source of salvation, you will find that He will never let you down. You are not the source of your righteousness or success.

Falling from grace is not about falling into sin, which is what people often think it is. Falling from grace happens when we try to perform for God's approval. We don't receive what we want and, as a result, we become bitter (Hebrews 12:15). People who depend on the law, or self-effort and good works, to justify themselves have fallen from grace, and Christ has become of no effect to them (Galatians 5:4).

The story of the prodigal son is a perfect example. When he returned home, his older brother became angry and refused to celebrate with him, despite their father's pleas. This older son was bitter because he felt that his hard work had qualified him for favor (Luke 15:28, 29). How many of us have taken this position in our relationship with

God? The older brother witnessed his younger brother receive undeserved favor and it made him angry! Their story shows us what happens when we expect our performance to win God's favor. When it doesn't, we feel condemned because we can never be enough; but under grace, we receive what we don't deserve.

The good news is that, in Jesus, you are secure from the failure that comes from self-effort. When it comes to the promises of God, we have to *always* and *only* consider Jesus, who was counted worthy of more glory than Moses (Hebrews 3:1-3). His sacrifice paved the way for us to have a bold position of favor with the Father and the ability to go before Him without a sense of guilt or fear. Jesus is greater than all others; He is greater than us or our own efforts. Therefore, everything that comes from Him is greater than anything that could ever come from us or anyone before us. The Law of Moses is not higher than the grace of God, which is why we should not use it as the standard against which we measure our walk with God.

Grace provides us with everything we need to live a godly and successful life. Everything that God has instructed for Christian living is possible because Jesus lives on the inside of us. He is constantly working in us to carry out His will and His good pleasure (Philippians 2:13). Grace empowers us to do what we cannot do in our own ability. The things that the world would consider impossible to accomplish in the way of godly living are fully possible with God. When we are under grace, we are no longer under the law, which means that sin cannot rule over us (Romans 6:14). We are free from our old nature and have the liberty to live godly lives. We are beneficiaries of the unmerited favor of God. This is the good news that sets us free from a performance-based type of Christianity. We can grow in a personal relationship with God, learning from Him every step of the way in spite of our flaws and allowing the Holy Spirit to teach us. We never have to experience the consequences of falling from grace when we rely on His finished works instead of ourselves.

# STUDY QUESTIONS

1. What does it mean to depend on Jesus for our salvation? ______

______

______

______

2. What did the Law of Moses dictate? ______

______

______

______

3. Accepting God's grace requires a willingness to ______

______

______.

4. What was the Law of Moses based on? ______

5. Why did Jesus come to the Earth? ______

______

______

______

6. True or False: The law constantly reminds us of our sin.

7. Why is the law unable to justify anyone? ________________________________

________________________________________________

________________________________________________

________________________________________________

8. True or False: Grace gives the believer a pass to sin when they feel weak in their faith.

9. What does it mean to fall from grace? ________________________________

________________________________________________

________________________________________________

________________________________________________

10. What is a result of continued self-effort to obtain God's approval? ____________

________________________________________________

________________________________________________

________________________________________________

# ANSWER KEY

1. to depend on what comes from Him, to depend on His finished works
2. that the people work hard to keep the entire law in order to escape death
3. abandon our self-effort
4. self-effort
5. to redeem everyone living under the law
6. True
7. because it brings the knowledge of sin
8. False
9. to depend on our self-effort instead of Jesus
10. bitterness and frustration due to constantly falling short

**SCRIPTURE REFERENCES**

John 1:17

2 Corinthians 3:7

John 20:30-32

Romans 11:6

Exodus 19:8

Matthew 5:17, 18

1 Corinthians 15:56

Galatians 4:4, 5

Romans 3:20

Titus 2:11, 12

Hebrews 12:15

Galatians 5:4

Luke 15:28, 29

Hebrews 3:1-3

Philippians 2:13

Romans 6:14

# CHAPTER EIGHTEEN
# LAYING HOLD OF THE PROMISES OF GOD

There is a reason why the finished works of Jesus Christ are not manifesting themselves in the lives of so many believers at the level and degree to which they should. Everything that we will ever need to live an abundant life has already been made available to us, but it requires faith in order to obtain those things in this natural, physical realm. Healing, deliverance, wholeness, and financial prosperity belong to us now, but receiving these things into our reality on a daily basis begins with accepting, by faith, that God has already given us everything we will ever need to live. Everything in the physical realm begins in the spiritual realm, so to experience physical blessings, we must receive spiritual blessings, first. These spiritual blessings are in Christ, and when Christ is in us, we realize that God has already placed what we need inside of us. Believing this strengthens our faith and positions us for manifestation.

Jesus didn't wait for you to get sick before providing healing. He didn't wait for you to be in lack financially before making sure the resources you need would be at your disposal. Through His foreknowledge, He already knew what you would need. This is a powerful truth! The location of all spiritual blessings is the heavenly realm, in Christ.

Since Christ lives in you, you already possess these amazing finished works. Pulling them out of the spiritual realm depends on your ability to exercise your faith to do so.

God set things up for the believer to function within His kingdom and to appropriate what He has done for each of us. Our faith is designed to possess what God's grace has made available. Grace makes and faith takes! This concept is really simple but elusive if you are still trying to operate according to self-effort (performing to try and get God to do something for you). The promises contained within the Bible are based on the finished works of Jesus, not your good works. Religion tells us to figure out how to get things from God, but grace says it is already supplied. We are saved, healed, delivered, and given access to the abundant, God-kind of life through grace, by faith.

God's divine power has given us everything pertaining to life and godliness, through the knowledge of Him who called us (2 Peter 1:3). God has literally blessed us with every single thing we would ever need to live overcoming, victorious lives that show forth His glory. He has blessed us with all spiritual blessings in heavenly places in Christ Jesus (Ephesians 1:3). Jesus bore our sins in His body on the cross so that we could die to sin and live to righteousness. We were healed by the wounds that Jesus suffered and, since we *were* healed, it means that we *are* healed right now (1 Peter 2:24). No more trying to get God to heal you when you meditate on the truth of your present possession of healing.

Faith is the substance of things hoped for, and the evidence of things not seen (Hebrews 11:1). It is vital to the life of a Christian because it is the spiritual currency that funnels what we cannot see in the spiritual realm into manifestation in the natural realm. *"Therefore it is of faith, that it might be by grace; to the end the promise might be sure to all the seed; not to that only which is of the law, but to that also which is of the faith of Abraham; who is the father of us all"* (Romans 4:16). Inheriting the blessing and promises of God is entirely dependent on your faith. For the unmerited favor of God to be manifested, we have to act in faith. What we can't see is real because we have evidence of it in the Word of God. Faith is the confirmation or title deed of what we are believing God for and it comes by hearing and comprehending the Word of God (Hebrews 11:1, *AMPC*; Romans 10:17).

Living a life of faith, as a believer, requires focus on God and His Word. Without allowing the Word to dictate your belief system, you will lose sight of what God has blessed you with in the spiritual realm. It is for this reason that consistent study and meditation of God's Word should be priority in your daily life. Doing this helps you to remain in a position of high faith, which enables you to more easily lay hold of the things God has freely given you in Christ.

With every attempt to get what grace has made available there is a fight, but the fight is a good one because it is already fixed for your victory (1 Timothy 6:12). You are not fighting to win; you are fighting because you have *already* won. You are existing from a place of victory, not fighting for the victory. When your faith is tried, it employs patience and builds your character (James 1:3, 4). The more highly developed you are in your faith, the quicker you will see results.

## THE RIGHTEOUSNESS-FAITH CONNECTION

One of the most important keys to receiving from God is knowing that you are the righteousness of God. In fact, faith and righteousness are closely linked. We are repeatedly instructed in the Word of God to live by faith, but it is difficult to believe God for things when you feel you are unrighteous or unworthy (Habakkuk 2:4; Galatians 3:11; Hebrews 10:38). Knowing your identity in Christ is critical to receiving what He has paid the price to give you.

As the righteousness of God, your way of living *is* faith. Romans 1:17 says that the just shall live by faith. To be just, according to the Scriptures, means to be made righteous. This is exactly what happened to you when you received Christ. Your spirit was infused with His righteousness, which is perfect. Knowing and believing this righteousness is the key to everything in your Christian walk. When you know you are the righteousness of God through Christ Jesus, it gives you a sense of confidence. You have a blood-bought right to come boldly to the throne of grace to receive help in a time of need and to have access to the unlimited provision of God (Hebrews 4:16; Philippians 4:19). Knowing you are righteous will prevent you from shrinking back from God and shrinking back from what He said you can have. The apostle Paul wrote that he lived by faith in Jesus Christ, who gave Himself for us (Galatians 2:20). This is also how we are to live (2 Corinthians 5:7).

Often we allow the devil to rob us of our faith and talk us out of what God has promised in His Word. The way to combat that is to position yourself to constantly be filled with the Word of God. Always remember that you have an adversary and you are in a war (1 Peter 5:8). The devil is not a fictitious character or vague concept; he is a real spiritual being who wants to undermine your faith at every turn. He can't eradicate what Jesus has secured for you, but he can slow down your progress and hinder certain things from coming to pass by attacking your faith. He hates to see your faith strengthened, but you have to commit to persevere. As believers, we do not allow our circumstances to dictate whether or not we believe what God said. We walk by the Word of God no matter what, refusing to trust our five senses to draw conclusions about what God is doing.

Joy comes from what you know from the Word of God because it strengthens you with the ammunition to overcome trials. This is different from happiness, which can change based on circumstances. Joy is a deep inward sense of well-being and conviction that God has done what He promised and there is no need to worry. No outward circumstance can cause joy to dissipate when you are grounded in the Word of God.

Making a quality decision not to cast away your confidence in God is vital (Hebrews 10:35). Many opportunities will come to abandon what God said in His Word, but don't give in to the devil's suggestions. We need patience to do God's will (Hebrews 10:36). Often the issue isn't that we are doing the wrong thing, but that we aren't doing the right thing *long enough.* The decision to stand on the Word long enough to see results will connect you to the grace needed to bring those promises to pass, to pull them out of the spiritual realm and into physical manifestation. Everything you need exists in the kingdom of God and Jesus has provided the ability to access those things through the grace of God. Your faith is the key to obtaining what grace has secured for you!

# STUDY QUESTIONS

1. What is the first step to seeing the promises of God manifest in your life? ______

______

______

______

2. True or False: Everything in the natural realm starts in the spiritual realm.

3. All spiritual blessings are in ______.

4. How does God want the believer to function in His kingdom? ______

______

______

______

5. The promises in the Word of God are based on ______.

6. Why is faith vital to thc Christian life? ______

______

______

______

7. True or False: Inheriting the promises of God is entirely dependent on your faith.

8. Why is knowing you are the righteousness of God critical to receiving the promises of God? ______________________________

______________________________

______________________________

______________________________

9. What is faith? ______________________________

______________________________

______________________________

______________________________

10. Often the issue isn't that we are doing the wrong thing, but that we are ______________

______________________________.

# ANSWER KEY

1. accepting, by faith, that God has already given you everything you will ever need to live
2. True
3. heavenly places in Christ
4. by using faith to appropriate what He has made available
5. the finished works of Jesus
6. because it is the currency through which all the promises of God are funneled from the spiritual realm into the natural realm
7. True
8. because when you know you are the righteousness of God it gives you confidence to boldly lay hold of God's promises
9. the substance of things hoped for, the evidence of things not seen
10. not doing the right thing long enough

**SCRIPTURE REFERENCES**

2 Peter 1:3

Ephesians 1:3

1 Peter 2:24

Hebrews 11:1

Romans 4:16

Hebrews 11:1, *AMPC*

Romans 10:17

1 Timothy 6:12

James 1:3, 4

Habakkuk 2:4

Galatians 3:11

Hebrews 10:38

Romans 1:17

Hebrews 4:16

Philippians 4:19

Galatians 2:20

2 Corinthians 5:7

1 Peter 5:8

Hebrews 10:35, 36

# CHAPTER NINETEEN
# HIGHLY DEVELOPED FAITH FOR QUICK MANIFESTATION

Developing our faith is vital to seeing the promises of God come to fruition in our lives. In fact, believers are supposed to be getting far more results than those who have not made Jesus their Lord and Savior. Unfortunately, many of us are not highly developed in the faith that God has given us and are more affected by what we experience with our five senses than we are in the principles of faith. The truth is that the more developed we are in something, the more quickly we are able to get results. If we want to pull our spiritual inheritance out of the realm of heaven and into the earth then we will have to become proficient in faith. The will of God is for all of His promises to consistently manifest in our lives. Our faith is the bridge that connects the spiritual to the physical.

When something is taken to the extreme, an imbalance is the inevitable result. When faith is taken to the extreme, it causes legalism. Conversely, when grace is taken to the extreme it causes passive Christianity. For effective results in the life of a believer, there must be a balance of grace and faith, with both working together in unison. Remember that faith and grace are closely linked. You can't have one without the other. We are saved by grace, through faith (Ephesians 2:8). Faith secures what grace has made available to us.

God never responds to prayers that ask Him to do what He has already done or what He has already asked us to do, but religion has trained us to go to Him from a position of need or incompletion. It is as if we are waiting for God to do something that He has given us the power and authority to command. When it comes to quickly manifesting the benefits of grace, Philemon 1:6 gives us some amazing insight: *"That the communication of thy faith may become effectual by the acknowledging of every good thing which is in you in Christ Jesus."* Everything we need and desire is in us because Jesus Christ is in us! Therefore, when we pray for God to give us healing or prosperity, we are actually delaying the answer to our prayer. The answer has already been given in Christ Jesus. It is our responsibility to appropriate the promises of God by acknowledging what we already possess through the finished works of Jesus. We use our faith to bring those things into natural manifestation. God has given us all that we could ever need in life, every moment of the day.

## THE CONFIDENCE OF THE RIGHTEOUS

Romans 4:16 says, *"Therefore it is of faith, that it might be by grace; to the end the promise might be sure to all the seed; not to that only which is of the law, but to that also which is of the faith of Abraham; who is the father of us all."* It is of faith that it might be by grace that the promise will be available to all future generations. This applies not only to those under the law, but also to those who have the faith of Abraham. Abraham's faith was unwavering and refused to bow to the circumstances. When we believe like him, it pulls the blessings of grace out of the spiritual realm and into the natural realm.

Faith in the grace of God to make us righteous through our belief in Jesus Christ is another key to the manifestation. It gives us confidence in who we are and what belongs to us now that we are in Him. We have been declared righteous by what Jesus did, but this is revealed to us in our natural life by faith. The righteousness of God is revealed from faith to faith, and the just (those declared righteous) shall live by faith (Romans 1:17; Hebrews 10:38). Because we are called to live a life of faith as God's people, it displeases Him when we do not accept this truth. We are to fight the good fight of faith and claim eternal life, to which we were called as believers (1 Timothy 6:12).

The fight that God calls us to is the fight to maintain our position on what faith says is ours by grace. The enemy will oppose us in this fight, but our faith must remain strong by continually feeding it with the Word of God. Because faith comes by hearing the Word of God, the more we hear, the more faith comes (Romans 10:17). Faith and the Word are one. The Word strengthens our faith and allows us to take possession of what grace has already made available.

When we truly believe what God said in His Word, and that belief is rooted in our hearts, we rest. In fact, resting is the highest kind of faith because it communicates that we believe the work is completed, we possess our inheritance, and it is making its way to us as we rest. The more proficient we become in resting in the promises of God, the quicker we will see things begin to come to pass. While we rest, we want to use our words to release the creative power of God into our circumstances. We have what we say all the time, and when we only speak the Word of God, that is what we will see manifest in our lives. Murmuring and complaining demonstrate the opposite of faith and rest. When we truly rest, we eliminate any words from our vocabulary and speech that do not line up with the Word of God.

Still another key to seeing quick manifestations is to remain the same in faith about the promises of God and not waver. An unshakeable truth is that God supplies our needs every day (Philippians 4:19). It doesn't matter what it looks like because our needs are already met. We should never change what we are saying, thinking, or standing on just because things appear to be contrary. When we begin to flow in a consistency of faith, we will see things begin to happen at a more rapid rate.

## HOPE THAT IS UNSHAKEABLE

Faith in grace gives us the sure hope of a life in Christ. Everyone has been given *the* measure of faith and we receive that measure when we are born again (Romans 12:3). Faith is the confirmation of what we hope for, and the conviction of its reality, regardless of what we see or do not see (Hebrews 11:1, *AMPC*). Hope is the earnest expectation of something, but faith is the "stuff" that fills the hope with tangible substance.

Since faith comes by hearing the Word of God, the Word has to be our highest priority. The devil has a strategy every day to steal, kill, and destroy our lives, which is why we cannot successfully maintain our victory over him if we are not filled with the Word of God (John 10:10). In order to see those quick manifestations we desire, we must maintain an undisturbed focus on the Word of God and allow it to shape the way we think, speak, and walk as Christians. If we stop living by the Word, we stop living. Manifestations come when we give the Word first place in our lives.

What are the good things that we possess that we have a right to see materialize in our lives as sons and daughters of God? The faith of God, the righteousness of God, the healing, restoration, deliverance, wisdom, and glory of God. In Christ, we are walking powerhouses of God's ability. We contain within our spirits the keys and resources necessary to be completely provided for in every area of our lives (John 6:63). Developing faith in this truth is the key to quick manifestations and harvests.

God honors acts of faith. When we act on the Word of God, going beyond simply hearing it and then forgetting it, we will be blessed. James 1:25 says, "*But whoso looketh into the perfect law of liberty, and continueth therein, he being not a forgetful hearer, but a doer of the work, this man shall be blessed in his deed.*" When you look into the Word of God, it is important to continue in the things you have learned and are learning. This is key to seeing blessings and favors because then you become a consistent doer of the work of God.

Inheriting the promises of God is the outcome of faith, but these things are given as an act of grace on God's part (Romans 4:16). God quickens the dead, and calls all things that are not as though they were (Romans 4:17). When we begin calling things that do not exist as if they did, we are imitating God and putting our faith to work. Faith in grace will compel us to open our mouths and decree the Word of God in our lives. These are the keys to seeing fast results while simultaneously building our faith. We must know who we are in Christ, know what we possess through grace, and believe that we have the power to access all the benefits of salvation by faith. Rapid and successive manifestations of grace can and should be the believer's reality every day!

# STUDY QUESTIONS

1. True or False: The more developed you are in something, the more quickly you can get results.

2. The works of the law are based on ________________________________.

3. True or False: Faith and grace don't always work together.

4. It is through God's __________________________ that we are born again.

5. What does it mean to be called "the just"? __________________________

6. What is the fight of faith? _____________________________________

7. What does the Word do for our faith? ______________________________

_____________________________________________

_____________________________________________

_____________________________________________

8. What does faith in grace give us? ______________________________

_____________________________________________

_____________________________________________

_____________________________________________

9. Faith is the ______________________________

_____________________________________________

_____________________________________________

_____________________________________________.

10. What is a way that we can begin to see quick manifestations? ______________

_____________________________________________

_____________________________________________

_____________________________________________

# ANSWER KEY

1. True
2. self-effort
3. False
4. unmerited favor
5. It means you have been declared righteous by God through faith in Jesus Christ.
6. maintaining our position on what faith says is ours by grace
7. It strengthens it.
8. the sure hope of a life in Christ
9. the confirmation of what we hope for, and the conviction of its reality, regardless of what we see or do not see
10. by calling those things that be not as though they were, just like God does

**SCRIPTURE REFERENCES**

Ephesians 2:8
Philemon 1:6
Romans 4:16
Romans 1:17
Hebrews 10:38
1Timothy 6:12
Philippians 4:19
Romans 10:17
Romans 12:3
Hebrews 11:1, *AMPC*
John 6:63
James 1:25
Romans 4:16, 17

# CHAPTER TWENTY
# ENHANCING THE FLOW OF GOD'S GRACE

The covenant of grace requires one thing of us: belief. In fact, the flow of grace in our lives is only possible when we release the idea of having to work to make God do something for us. His grace is His unmerited favor working on our behalf. Believers are to believe the Word of God and believe in the finished works of Jesus. True humility is submitting to the Word of God and whatever He is telling you to do at any given time. Pride, on the other hand, is a refusal to submit to the Word. When we operate in pride, we put ourselves in a position for God to actively resist those things that are taking us further away from Him. If we want to enhance the flow of God's grace in our lives, we must maintain a posture of humility.

First Peter 5:5-7 says, *"Likewise, ye younger, submit yourselves unto the elder. Yea, all of you be subject one to another, and be clothed with humility: for God resisteth the proud, and giveth grace to the humble. Humble yourselves therefore under the mighty hand of God, that he may exalt you in due time: Casting all your care upon him; for he careth for you."* In this passage, Peter is teaching on the concept of submission. Just as the elders submit to the chief shepherd, those younger should submit to the elders. He calls this being "clothed" in humility.

To submit is to get under the mission of someone else or something else. We want to remain in the position to receive God's unmerited favor; and submission to God's Word is the key. The grace that we receive for our specific situations is proportionate to the level of humility that we walk in. It is not a matter of earning grace through humility. Humility is a voluntary position and it is in that position that we will find grace.

Pride is dangerous because it will not allow you to find the grace you need in a time of trouble. There is no grace to be found in self-effort or trying to do things your own way. In fact, grace will never be found in the life of an individual who thinks his or her way is the best way and refuses to receive God's instruction and direction. First Peter 5:6 instructs us to humble ourselves under the mighty hand of God so that He may exalt us in due time. Humbling ourselves is a voluntary act; God doesn't do it for us. We must make the decision as an act of our will to bring ourselves into a place of submission to God's Word.

In order to submit to God, we have to know what the Word of God says. It is impossible to submit to what you don't know. In essence, you have to be a Word addict! Something happens in your spirit and soul when you hear the Word and *keep* hearing it. When someone else has to humble you, it is humiliation; but when you humble yourself, God will exalt you.

Proverbs 15:33 says, "*The fear of the Lord is the instruction of wisdom; and before honour is humility.*" The fear of the Lord is referring to respecting, reverencing, and honoring God. When we walk in this reverence, honor is given to us by God, Himself; but when we walk in pride, we are setting ourselves up for a fall (Proverbs 18:12). The only way to get out of the situations we face is to submit to what God has said about those situations. Whether it is related to finances, relationships, or any other area, the answers we need are wrapped up in God's instructions to us in His written and spoken Word. When we humble ourselves under the direction of God in any given situation, we can escape the snares of the devil; but when we refuse to do things God's way and insist on doing things our own way, it leads to destruction (Proverbs 3:5-7). In every situation, we must ask ourselves, "What is the path of humility here? What does submitting to God's instruction here look like?" If we stay humble, we won't stay in the same place in life, but will experience greater levels of progress.

### HUMILITY AND REST GO HAND IN HAND

Resting in God is an act of humility. In fact, you can't have one without the other. Trust, reliance, and belief fall into the category of being humble. Everyone has cares and concerns in life, but true humility is resting in the finished works of Jesus so that His grace can flow uninterrupted and unhindered. To rest in the finished works of Christ means casting our cares on Jesus, knowing that everything we will ever need in this life has already been provided for. Doing this truly reflects humility. Worry, care, and walking in our own understanding are expressions of pride. When we are carrying the cares of this life, we are trying to make things work by our own power. Unfortunately, pride keeps grace from working because, where we lack submission to God's Word, we will lack grace.

There are so many areas in which we have the opportunity to walk in pride. We must make a quality decision to seek the wisdom of God's Word and submit to it so that we can experience His grace flowing in our lives. Without humility there is no honor, but when we humble ourselves we position ourselves for promotion.

# STUDY QUESTIONS

1. What does the covenant of grace require of us? ______________________

2. When is the flow of grace possible in our lives? ______________________
______________________
______________________
______________________

3. What is true humility? ______________________
______________________
______________________
______________________

4. Pride is a refusal to ______________________.

5. True or False: The grace we receive for our specific situations is proportionate to the level of humility that we walk in.

6. In order to submit to God, we must ______________________
______________________.

7. True or False: Humbling ourselves is a voluntary act.

8. How can we escape the snares of the devil? ______________________

______________________________________________

______________________________________________

______________________________________________

9. True or False: Resting in God is an act of humility.

10. ________________ and ________________ are expressions of pride.

# ANSWER KEY

1. belief
2. when we release the idea of working to get God to do something for us
3. submitting to the Word of God
4. submit to the Word of God
5. True
6. know what the Word of God says
7. True
8. by humbling ourselves under the direction of God in any given situation
9. True
10. Worry; care

**SCRIPTURE REFERENCES**

1 Peter 5:5-7

Proverbs 15:33

Proverbs 18:12

Proverbs 3:5-7

# CHAPTER TWENTY-ONE
# HOW TO FIND GRACE IN A TIME OF NEED

The grace of God is mandatory in the life of a believer. It is God's unmerited favor working on our behalf, doing what we could never do in our own ability. In order to get into this flow of grace, however, we must position ourselves to receive what God has for us by remaining humble. It is never God's fault when we don't receive His grace for certain situations in our lives. The flow is always going forth. The issue is whether or not we are in the right location, and that location is the place of humility.

James 4:6 says that God resists the proud but gives grace to the humble. To resist something means to actively fight against it. The humble person is the one who will find grace; but those who persist in their ungodly ways, plans, and performance-based works will experience the Lord actively fighting against them. It is actually His love that is the motivating force behind His resistance of the proud. You see, God will always fight against that which takes you out of the position to receive grace. When you are moving in a place of pride, God is actively working to get you back into humility. He does this by making it difficult for you to continue in pride. He corrects those whom He loves (Proverbs 3:12).

When it comes to finding grace in a time of need, it is important that we submit to God's instructions and remove ourselves from situations that defy Him. Our sins are not imputed to us when we are made righteous through faith in Christ Jesus (Romans 4:8); but even though our sins are not charged to our eternal accounts, there are consequences for our actions. God's blessings cannot flow through sin, lies, and deceit any more than electricity can flow through rubber. Sin has consequences and, when we continue in disobedience, there are things that will be blocked or even stopped from manifesting in our lives. This is not about our internal state of righteousness being altered or messed up, but it is about disrupting the flow of grace that we need for successful living on a day to day basis. A believer who won't remove themselves from any situation that God is instructing them to leave is going to suffer the negative consequences of those sins.

Revelation 18:4 says that we are not to partake of others' sins so that we won't partake of their consequences. God doesn't want His sons and daughters to have to go through the repercussions that sin brings. That is why we must humble ourselves. *"Submit yourselves therefore to God. Resist the devil, and he will flee from you. Draw nigh to God, and he will draw nigh to you"* (James 4:7, 8). Simultaneously submitting and resisting will get the devil to flee. In fact, we can't truly do one without the other. We actively fight against the devil by submitting to God with unflinching conviction. Resisting is not a passive activity, but instead it involves all of our faculties. We must draw near to God. In doing so, we cultivate an intimate relationship with Him. By refusing to submit to the devil and instead choosing to submit to God, we grow closer to God and begin to know Him in ways that we never did before. This intimacy cannot be achieved when we go along with the devil's words and ways of doing things.

As a loving Father, God is committed to ensuring that we don't drift away from Him. For this reason, He actively resists anything in our lives that draws us out of fellowship. He will not just stand by and allow the enemy to steal us away, but He will fight for us. When we humble ourselves, He lifts us up to a high place where the devil cannot touch us. The key is for us to cease from our own wisdom and ways of doing things. The wisdom we *think* we have about a situation may actually prevent us from receiving the grace that is available for us to overcome it. We have to ask ourselves if we are willing to let go of what we know for the sake of God's higher way of thinking (Proverbs 15:33). Humility is the conductor of the grace of God.

### PRIDE: A GRACE-BLOCKER

The reason pride is so dangerous is because it stops the grace of God like an insulator stops cold temperatures from getting in. When you are in a place of submitting to your plans and think what you want to do is greater than submission to what God wants to do, you are set up to fall from grace (Proverbs 18:12). Don't allow a prideful way of living to bring this fall to pass in your life. When you are in pride, you are overestimating who you are and exalting yourself above God's Word.

The only thing more powerful than Jesus Christ is each person's free moral agency. Your decision either to submit to God's way or submit to your way completely determines the way you're going to go. Can God show you what you don't know, take you where you've never been, and do with you what you've never done, or will you say, "I trust my way more"? The question is: will you voluntarily humble yourself under the Word or will you remain in pride? You will continue to go through the same issues over and over again until you step out of the center of things and make God's Word your final authority. Grace can never show up for the person who is intent on maintaining their agenda over God's agenda.

The destruction that is associated with remaining in pride is guaranteed (Proverbs 16:18). In fact, when situations and circumstances take place that clearly have destruction attached to them, back up and locate where pride entered the picture. Pride deceives (Obadiah 1:3). The pride of our own hearts and the pride associated with all of our plans and programs can trick us into thinking that our way is best; but the only way to success is to become hungry for what God is telling us to do. It takes humility to accept God's promotion. This means allowing our minds to be renewed by the truth of His Word. It also means we must become hungry for what God is telling us to do. In doing so, we will always find the grace to help us in our time of need.

# STUDY QUESTIONS

1. How do we get into the flow of grace? ____________________

____________________

____________________

____________________

2. God resists the ____________________, but gives grace to the ____________________.

3. What is the motivating force behind God resisting the proud? ____________________

____________________

____________________

____________________

4. True or False: God makes it difficult for you to continue in pride.

5. How do we find grace in a time of need? ____________________

____________________

____________________

____________________

6. True or False: Sin can affect our righteousness.

7. God fights for us when we ______________________________.

8. Why is pride so dangerous? ______________________________

______________________________

______________________________

______________________________

9. When are you set up to fall from grace? ______________________________

______________________________

______________________________

______________________________

10. What is the only thing more powerful than Jesus Christ? ______________________________

______________________________

# ANSWER KEY

1. by humbling ourselves
2. proud; humble
3. His love
4. True
5. submit to God's instructions and remove ourselves from situations that defy God
6. False
7. drift away from Him
8. It stops the grace of God.
9. When you submit to your plans and what you want to do instead of what God wants you to do
10. free moral agency

**SCRIPTURE REFERENCES**

James 4:6-8
Proverbs 3:12
Romans 4:8
Revelation 18:4
Proverbs 15:33
Proverbs 18:12
Proverbs 16:18
Obadiah 1:3

# CHAPTER TWENTY-TWO
# HOW TO SUBMIT

Resting in God is something that many Christians have not mastered because it has become the norm to carry the cares of this life. However, God never designed us to carry care or worry about anything. To rest is to have confidence in the finished works of Jesus Christ. The best way to illustrate the type of rest that God wants us to have as it relates to Him is to think of a chair. When you go to sit in a chair, you don't give any thought to whether that chair is going to hold you. You simply take a seat! There is a confident trust in that chair's ability to hold you when you sit down. This is the same way God wants us rest in Him. We must "take a seat" and allow Him to do what He does best—take care of us. When we choose to enter into God's rest, we are demonstrating humility and allowing His grace to flow in our lives.

Hebrews 4:6 says, "*Seeing therefore it remaineth that some must enter therein, and they to whom it was first preached entered not in because of unbelief.*" God wants us to enter in, but it is difficult for Him to do things for us when we aren't at rest. When we have unbelief in the finished works of Jesus and refuse to put our trust in God, we cut ourselves off from the rest that sustains us and gets results. We simply cannot assume the position of trying to work things out on our own any longer. The place of rest is the place of manifestation. The position of rest is the evidence of true belief. When you think about your life, situations, and circumstances, are you at rest? Are you at peace? Will you believe God or not? If you believe what Jesus has promised, that it is already finished, you will be at rest.

In order to become established in the position of rest, we must meditate on the promises found in the Word of God more than on the problems that we face. Meditating on the Word will actually escort us into the rest. Hebrews 4:11 says, *"Let us labour therefore to enter into that rest, lest any man fall after the same example of unbelief."* As believers, our work is the labor that it takes to enter the rest; that's when the finished works become a reality in our lives. We must always remember that we are covenant recipients of God's grace and the devil will use anything he can to keep us out of rest. Spiritual warfare is maintaining a position of rest in the victory that Jesus died to obtain.

Just like the illustration of the chair shows us, we are able to rest in that which we have confidence. There is no rest without confidence. *"Cast not away therefore your confidence, which hath great recompence of reward"* (Hebrews 10:35). Many times it is simply a matter of actually working our faith in the Word long enough to see it bring about a change in our lives. When we commit to submitting to the Word of God in every area of life, we will find ourselves trusting in it more and more, which will cause us to rest in what Jesus has already done for us.

### SIX WORKS OF FAITH

In order to get into a place of rest, there are six works of faith that are a part of the "labor" God has called us to as believers:

1. **We must renew our minds with the Word of God.**

   After getting born again, the most important thing to do is renew the mind. *"And be not conformed to this world: but be ye transformed by the renewing of your mind, that ye may prove what is that good, and acceptable, and perfect, will of God"* (Romans 12:2). Getting saved isn't enough; we have to allow the Word to change the way we think. Without new information guiding our lives, we are destined to make the same decisions, live in the same fear, and be subject to the same conditions that governed our lives before receiving Christ. We must make a quality decision to humble ourselves under the instruction of God and allow the Word to change our thinking, not the other way around. Renewing the mind is a lifetime process that positions us to be able to rest in the finished works of Jesus on a daily basis.

2. **We must confess the Word of God.**

   Confession of God's Word is critical. We must develop the discipline of confessing what God has said about us because, as we do this, we fill our hearts and minds with its truth. This empowers us to get results in life. When we speak the Word of God, we are engaging the creative power of God and pulling things out of the spiritual realm and into the natural realm where we can see them.

3. **We must meditate on God's Word.**

   Meditating on the Word of God is another work of faith that should be a part of every believer's life. To meditate is to mutter, ponder, and turn the Word over in our minds again and again until it begins to change the way we think. We are to consider the Word of God until we can see ourselves doing it. Joshua 1:8 says to meditate on the Word day and night in order to make our way prosperous and have good success. The manifestation of what we meditate on will be seen by all, according to First Timothy 4:15.

4. **We must spend time in prayer.**

   Spending time with God and basking in His presence through prayer is a key to entering into His rest. When we pray, we are not begging Him to do something, but we are praising and thanking Him for what He has *already* done. In addition, praying in the Spirit builds us up and helps us keep our minds on Him, which also enables us to rest.

5. **We must hear the Word.**

   Faith comes by hearing the Word of God over and over again (Romans 10:17). When we listen to the Word preached and taught on a regular basis, we keep ourselves in the overflow spiritually, and our faith remains strong. Highly developed faith in God and the finished works of Jesus will give us the ability to overcome any challenge that we face. We can stay in a posture of rest when we position ourselves to hear the Word on a continual basis.

6. **We must believe the love of God for us.**

   It is impossible to rest in what God has done for us if we really don't believe that He loves us. When we believe God loves us, we will believe in the promises of God for us. Receiving anything from God is based on the foundation of believing in His love. Our confidence in God's love for us comes from meditating on His nature, character, and love found in the Scriptures.

Entering into God's rest requires labor on our part, but the labor is not based on self-effort. It comes from a desire to express our faith practically so that we can lay hold of what Jesus has done for us. Everything we do should come from the place of rest and trust in what God has already done, not us trying to get Him to do something. We can walk in a level of power and manifestation that has never been seen before when we humble ourselves and rest in God's ability, not our own. This is truly the only way to activate the promises of God in our lives.

# STUDY QUESTIONS

1. Why have many Christians not mastered resting in God? ______________________

______________________________________________________________

______________________________________________________________

______________________________________________________________

2. What does it mean to rest in God? ______________________________________

______________________________________________________________

______________________________________________________________

______________________________________________________________

3. True or False: It is difficult for God to do things for us when we are not at rest.

4. The place of rest is the place of ____________________________________.

5. What is the evidence of true belief? ____________________________________

6. We must not cast away our ____________________________________.

7. What are the six works of faith? ____________________

____________________

____________________

____________________

# ANSWER KEY

1. because it has become the norm to carry the cares of this life
2. to have confidence in the finished works of Jesus
3. True
4. manifestation
5. rest
6. confidence
7. renewing the mind; confessing the Word of God; meditating on the Word of God; spending time in prayer; hearing the Word of God; and believing the love of God for us

**SCRIPTURE REFERENCES**

Hebrews 4:6, 11
Hebrews 10:35
Romans 12:2
Joshua 1:8
1 Timothy 4:15
Romans 10:17

# CHAPTER TWENTY-THREE
# ENTERING INTO GOD'S REST

Did you know that as a son or daughter of God, your inheritance in Christ includes rest that surpasses anything you could imagine? God wants to give rest to whoever is weary and burdened, but finding this rest is based on whether or not we believe His grace has made it available to us. We see the promise of this rest for the believer in the Old Testament, and we realize it is a shadow of the future. Following this theme through to the New Testament, we learn that Jesus, in fact, is our rest because He has already secured everything we will ever need to live an abundant life. All that is required for us to reach the point of resting in Him is simply to trust and believe what God tells us in His Word. If we are willing to receive what He has for us, we will enter into His rest (Hebrews 4:9-11).

The Gospel is the Good News about God's unmerited favor that has been made available to us through Christ Jesus. The greatest faith a person can have is to rest in what Jesus has done. The truth about entering into God's rest is too important for us to overlook, misinterpret, or overcomplicate. It is sometimes difficult to fathom that everything we need has already been taken care of and that we don't have to rely on our own self-effort to obtain it, but the truth is that God has done all the work. Our labor is to rest in the finished works. We must resist the temptation to think we can do what God has already done. The idea of simply receiving something that has already been done seems almost too good to be true, but this Good News is what Jesus wants us to grab hold of.

When it comes to the rest God has made available to us, the Bible says that we must *"fear, lest, a promise being left us of entering into his rest, any of you should seem to come short of it"* (Hebrews 4:1). Here, the word "fear" means to be cautious, aware, and diligent. In this context, resting means to rely on, have confidence in, and trust what God already did. Again, the highest form of faith we can have is to rest, but resting is not the same thing as doing nothing. It does not mean being idle. When we are resting in the finished works of Jesus we are constantly utilizing our faith to lay hold of those finished works. We are making sure that our words, thoughts, and actions correspond with what we say we believe, even when circumstances look contrary. We are rejecting all suggestions from the enemy that try to present facts that contradict what Jesus has done. This is the labor God is talking about. This is the "work" that is involved with pressing into the rest that God has provided for us.

The Gospel was preached to all, but those who did not hear it in faith did not profit from it (Hebrews 4:2). All of God's works have been finished since the foundation of the world, but it is our faith that draws them out of the spiritual realm and into natural manifestation. We rest because the works are finished. When we maintain our peace and our rest, we will prosper in everything that we do.

## A SHADOW OF THINGS TO COME

The issue of the Sabbath is very significant to new-covenant believers. Often when we hear about the Sabbath, the assumption is that it is referring to a specific day in which we are to refrain from all work. While this is true under the Law of Moses, and while there is a definite value in setting aside a day of the week to rest, under the dispensation of grace the Sabbath is not what we think it is. From a big picture standpoint, the Old Testament was a shadow of who was to come later. *Jesus* is actually our Sabbath now. The Law of Moses instructed the people to remember the Sabbath day, to keep it holy (Exodus 20:8). The idea was to work six days and rest on the seventh as a way of commemorating the fact that God made all of creation in six days and rested on the seventh (Exodus 20:10-11). But even beyond the observance of a day of the week to rest, Jesus is our ultimate rest. He provides us with the rest we need from self-effort because He has done everything that will ever need to be done to secure our righteousness. Because of this understanding of Jesus as our Sabbath rest, we don't have to allow ourselves to be judged by anyone about whether we observe the Sabbath on a particular day or not (Colossians 2:16).

The Word of God says that there are some to whom the Gospel was preached who did not enter into God's rest because of their unbelief (Hebrews 3:18, 19). Even today, some people still struggle because they do not believe that everything they need is already finished and waiting to be claimed. Whenever you start adding "steps" to what Jesus has already done, you are essentially saying that He is not enough. We must make a quality decision to acknowledge and rest in what He has already done. In fact, if you aren't resting, you are actually in unbelief. Religion says that we have to work to try and finish what Jesus has completed, but the only work that remains for us is to enter into His rest. It is labor for us to resist what the world tells us and deliberately agree with what God says. There remains a rest for God's people, and those who enter into it have ceased from their own efforts. Our daily goal is to press into this rest at all costs and refuse to allow anything to move us from our resting position (Hebrews 4:5-11).

It is really important not to return to the bondage of self-effort. As believers, we have been made to sit with Christ in heavenly places (Ephesians 2:6). How well you sit and rest will determine how well you walk and live. Faith is the currency that we must use to enter into God's rest. It is not always easy to rest when circumstances and situations are challenging our mind and emotions, but when we truly believe in the finished works of Jesus, we are free to receive what God wants to give us.

> And it shall be, when the Lord thy God shall have brought thee into the land which he sware unto thy fathers, to Abraham, to Isaac, and to Jacob, to give thee great and goodly cities, which thou buildedst not, And houses full of all

good things, which thou filledst not, and wells digged, which thou diggedst not, vineyards and olive trees, which thou plantedst not; when thou shalt have eaten and be full; Then beware lest thou forget the Lord, which brought thee forth out of the land of Egypt, from the house of bondage (Deuteronomy 6:10-12).

Always remember that these promises from God are not based on self-effort, but on belief in God's faithfulness (2 Timothy 2:13). In other words, there is nothing you could ever do to qualify for God's goodness in your life. This is why you aren't disqualified when you miss the mark. God's grace is sufficient and has already secured your abundance. When Jesus met the Samaritan woman at the well, He told her about the living water He had to offer (John 4:10). He later told His disciples that He had meat they did not know about (John 4:32). Compared to what Jesus has for us, what we can offer Him is null and void. We have to draw from Him, alone, not our own efforts, and let Him minister to us. In fact, when we draw from Jesus, it nourishes Him! Our job is not to go into self-effort mode, but to sit at the feet of Jesus, rest, draw from Him, and then go out and serve others (Luke 10:38-42). Whether it is the revelation of entering into the rest of God or sharing any of God's promises, spiritually we must put ourselves in position to be Jesus' hands and feet in the earth (Matthew 10:8).

God wants us to receive all that He has to give us so that we become demonstrations of how to rest and receive by faith. Every day is an opportunity to enter into His rest and stay there. We can pour into other people from the overflow that we receive from our time spent with the Lord (Acts 20:35). Jesus came to minister and give His life for us so that we could rest in His finished works and receive the benefits of abundant life by faith (Matthew 20:28). This is the labor of the believer and the avenue through which we can become examples to the world of what it means to receive God's grace.

# STUDY QUESTIONS

1. What is finding the rest of God based on? ______

2. True or False: The Old Testament foreshadowed the rest that is available to believers today.

3. How do we rest in Jesus? ______

4. Who are the ones who don't profit from the Gospel? ______

5. What does the word “fear” mean in Hebrews 4:1-4? ______________________

________________________________________________

________________________________________________

________________________________________________

6. True or False: Believers are obligated to observe a particular day for the Sabbath.

7. What is the believer’s only work today? ______________________

________________________________________________

________________________________________________

________________________________________________

8. True or False: We have to offer Jesus a lot in return for what He did for us.

9. Why did Jesus come? ______________________

________________________________________________

________________________________________________

________________________________________________

# ANSWER KEY

1. whether we believe that His grace has made rest available to us
2. True
3. by being willing to receive what He has for us
4. those who don't hear it in faith
5. to be cautious, aware, and diligent
6. False
7. to labor to enter into God's rest
8. False
9. to minister to and serve others

**SCRIPTURE REFERENCES**

Hebrews 4:1, 2, 5-11
Exodus 20:8, 10, 11
Colossians 2:16
Hebrews 3:18, 19
Ephesians 2:6
Deuteronomy 6:10-12
2 Timothy 2:13
John 4:10, 32
Luke 10:38-42
Matthew 10:8
Acts 20:35
Matthew 20:28

# CHAPTER TWENTY-FOUR
# POSITIONING YOURSELF FOR GOD'S PROMISES

If you knew the key to receiving every one of God's promises for your life, would you use it? Most people would answer that question with a resounding, "Yes!" There is a way to access everything the Bible promises you, and it is found in a simple concept: rest. This is something that often eludes most people because we believe that our lives and our success depend on our own self-effort. However, the greatest level of faith that we can experience comes when we choose to rest in the finished works of Jesus Christ, and have confidence in what He has already done. We must realize that we need God and that what we do on our own is not enough for us to see divine manifestations in our lives. When this realization becomes a reality, we will find ourselves in a place of humility where God is able to do exceedingly, abundantly more than we could ever ask or think (Ephesians 3:20). Because we have no idea what the future holds, we must have faith that He will show us the way on our Christian walk. It is no easy task to resist what the world tells us and believe God, but when we fully trust Him in any situation, we enter into the rest He has promised us.

It is difficult to rest in God sometimes because it goes against every human tendency we have to make things happen on our own. We tend to want to trust in our own ability and employ self-effort in an attempt to get results. One problem with this is that it is based in pride and, if the truth be told, we get a sense of entitlement and even self-righteousness when we feel like we did it ourselves. Well, this is exactly the attitude that God wants us to get rid of. *He* wants the glory and the credit for the wonderful things that happen in our lives. He wants to bring us to a place of completely trusting and relying on Him for everything. As our divine guide, God wants to lead us through life and bring us to a place of absolute dependence on Him. This is actually a great relief for us because it allows us to cease from our own labor and, consequently, the pride that comes from personal accomplishment. We can completely immerse ourselves in the finished works of Jesus and keep ourselves from the self-focus that can distract us from Him and make us feel like failures when things don't go as we had hoped. Putting all our trust in God takes a tremendous amount of pressure off of us.

Because of the uncertainty of life, with all of its twists and turns, it is imperative that we allow God to lead us in every situation (Jeremiah 10:23). We need Him to guide us. Life is a vapor that appears for a while and then disappears (James 4:14). Believers must purposely and intentionally confess with their mouths the Word of God, which is the will of God. It is not up to us to decide where we will be, or what we will do in the future. We need God's leadership every step of the way. If we try to improve ourselves and our spiritual condition through our own efforts, we will experience the same level of living that we always have. We cannot get the God-kind of results unless God, Himself, is working.

*"Let us therefore fear, lest, a promise being left us of entering into his rest, any of you should seem to come short of it"* (Hebrews 4:1). This reference to fear is not speaking of being afraid of danger. Instead, it is talking about being cautious, aware, and diligent so that we do not miss out on what God has for us. When God promised the people a land for which they did not work, cities they didn't build, and vineyards and olive yards to eat from which they did not plant, He was letting them know that all of these things were based on His grace, not what they labored and worked for themselves (Deuteronomy 6:10-12; Joshua 24:13). This concept is difficult for the natural mind to

receive but it is the way God wants us to relate to Him. All that was required for the Israelites to claim those blessings was to rest and the same is true for us.

Many of the things we see in the Old Testament are a type and shadow of what was to come, and the posture of rest that God wanted His people to take back then is also how He wants us to function today. As believers who are on the receiving end of everything God has prepared for us, we don't have to work for the blessing. God set the system up so that He completed the work. All we have to do is receive and rest. The promised land of goodness in the Old Testament is also an illustration of the goodness of salvation that is wrapped up in Jesus Christ. We can't earn righteousness or work our way into the new birth. These things are received by faith in Jesus alone, by trusting that He paid the ultimate price for you and me to have a right to be called sons and daughters of God. We are made righteous because of Him, not because of ourselves. It was not because of our own efforts or because we did anything to deserve it. God's goodness and grace are expressions of His love for us. Our task is to rest.

## MAINTAIN YOUR POSITION OF REST

Staying in a resting posture spiritually, mentally, and emotionally is definitely challenging at times. When bills are due, the pressure is on, and things are challenging your physical senses, there is a natural tendency to be moved from your rest. The world will contradict what God says to us about all of this because its way of doing things is completely opposed to the way God operates. It takes tenacity and a commitment to stand on the Word of God in order to believe what God has said, no matter what. This is where the labor comes into play. We must labor to enter into God's rest, lest anyone fall through unbelief (Hebrews 4:11). The truth is that we will hear things contrary to God's Word every day. We will see things that challenge our faith. We will be tempted to give up on our faith and lose sight of the fact that we already have everything we need for a good life. We must labor to believe what the Word tells us and reject what the world says. This will be a work of faith for every believer who is determined to receive what God has for them. In essence, this work of faith is when we agree with what God says at all costs, refusing to allow any other information to influence us. This work is different from the works of the law, which are based on our own self efforts.

Laboring to enter into His rest also means casting all of our cares on Him, because He cares for us (1 Peter 5:7). We have to believe this strongly enough to actually do so! The devil will attack us on this point, and try to shake our faith in God's love for us, but we can resist Him by keeping the Word of God in our mouths at all times. When Satan injects a thought into our minds that is designed to get us to take on the care of a particular issue or get us to worry, that is when we have to push back. This is the labor. We have to open our mouths and cast those thoughts down. It may take doing this several times a day, throughout the day, in order to get those thoughts to submit to the Word of God, but it will yield the desired results if we refuse to give in to the devil's lies and instead stay focused on what God has said.

Letting go of our cares, fears, and anxieties depends greatly on how well we learn to rest in Him. We will always have opportunities to become anxious, nervous, or fearful, but it is during those times that we can look to Jesus as our example. He always demonstrated a calm demeanor when He was dealing with situations where people were pulling on Him for miracles. He refused to be moved by situations and circumstances that rattled His disciples. Whether it was a raging storm while He was in a boat in the middle of the sea (Mark 4:35-41), or a crowd of hungry people who needed food, situations did not move Him to doubt what His heavenly Father would do (Matthew 14:13-21; Mark 6:33-44; Luke 9:11-17; John 6:2-14). He stayed focused on the Father and gave thanks for what was available to Him, and the supernatural always showed up. As believers, we can access the supernatural just like Jesus did by maintaining our position of rest in Him. God keeps those in perfect peace whose minds are calm, undisturbed, and intently focused on Him (Isaiah 26:3). This place of absolute rest and trust in God is the place where we will experience the answers to our prayers and the actualization of our faith. It is the pathway to miraculous results that become our way of life as children of God!

# STUDY QUESTIONS

1. The greatest level of faith we can experience comes when ____________________

   ________________________________________.

2. True or False: What we do on our own can get us to see divine manifestations.

3. What is the challenging part about resting in God? ____________________

   ________________________________________

   ________________________________________

   ________________________________________

4. How can we enter into the rest God has promised us? ____________________

   ________________________________________

   ________________________________________

   ________________________________________

5. Why is it important to verbally confess God's Word? ____________________

   ________________________________________

   ________________________________________

   ________________________________________

6. If we try to improve our lives through self-effort, what will be the result? ________

7. What were the promises God made to His people in Joshua 24:13 based on? ________

8. What was required for the people to receive these promises? ________

9. What is the real work of the believer? ________

10. Where do we find manifestations from God? ________

# ANSWER KEY

1. we can rest in the finished works of Jesus Christ
2. False
3. to resist what the world tells us and believe Him
4. by fully trusting Him in every situation
5. because God's Word is His will
6. We will stay in the same place in life.
7. His grace
8. rest
9. to labor to enter into the rest
10. in the place of rest

**SCRIPTURE REFERENCES**

Ephesians 3:20
Jeremiah 10:23
James 4:14
Hebrews 4:1, 11
Deuteronomy 6:10-12
Joshua 24:13
1 Peter 5:7
Mark 4:35-41
Matthew 14:13-21
Mark 6:33-44
Luke 9:11-17
John 6:2-14
Isaiah 26:3

# CHAPTER TWENTY-FIVE
# THE PRACTICAL SIDE OF TRUST

When it comes to entering into God's rest, there is an element of trust that must be present in the heart and mind of a believer. It is simply not possible to say we trust God without evidence, which is why we have to be able to authenticate our trust in Him. When we trust in God, we lean on Him confidently; but if we have confidence solely in ourselves, we will not last very long when trials, temptations, and the pressures of life knock on our doors. If we do not realize our need for God in every situation in life, we will end up in failure. God is our source and we must begin to develop this trust in Him long before trouble hits. Cultivating a lifestyle of trusting God happens when we depend on Him in the seemingly small things, every day. The more we involve Him in every aspect of our lives, trusting Him for all things great and small, the more our faith will be empowered and we will be able to believe and trust God for everything. This is truly the lifestyle of a believer.

As our heavenly Father, God wants us to trust Him enough to rest in His promises. This is the ultimate key to a successful and fruitful Christian life. The truth is that life is fleeting and we don't know what will happen tomorrow (James 4:14, 15). However, there is something and someone we can rely on in every season of life, no matter what is going on around us. God and His Word are infallible and we can never go wrong when we put our trust in Him and maintain unwavering confidence in the finished works of Jesus Christ. Make no mistake about it, we need God's guidance every step of the way. We cannot improve ourselves through our own efforts and He doesn't want us trying to do so in our own ability. We have a Savior who has already done all the work. It is time to rest in what He has done so that we can experience the supernatural kingdom lifestyle that God has secured through His grace.

The Word of God says that we need to be cognizant of the need to rest in the finished works of Jesus or else we will never come into the fullness of His promises. The Bible calls it "fear" in Hebrews 4:1, but it is not fear in the sense of being afraid of a bad outcome. It simply means that we are to be cautious, aware, and diligent to cultivate and maintain a sustained position of rest at all times, no matter what we are facing. This is actually where the labor of the believer lies. Our labor is not required to *receive* His blessings, but to resist the temptation to get into worry, doubt, and unbelief when contradictory circumstances or ideas present themselves to our minds. This is the work that we must commit to every single day.

The Old Testament is a type and shadow of things that would come later, and it provides a picture of how God wants us to view His blessings. *"And I have given you a land for which ye did not labour, and cities which ye built not, and ye dwell in them; of the vineyards and oliveyards which ye planted not do ye eat"* (Joshua 24:13). This is the equivalent of the finished works of Christ today. Now all of these things were already prepared for the people and waiting for them to take possession of them. God also told the people not to forget Him when He brought them into their promised land (Deuteronomy 6:10-12). The same is true for us today. There are promises and blessings that are waiting for us, but we must labor to enter into this rest and avoid getting into unbelief (Hebrews 4:11). We are to keep in remembrance the redemptive work of Christ that made all these wonderful blessings available to us. God wants us to always keep Him at the forefront of our minds. When we think of Him it should invoke peace and security in what He has already done.

Keep in mind that rest does not mean inactivity. This is where a lot of believers miss it. We are still to go about our daily lives, doing the things we are called to do and taking care of our responsibilities. However, while we are doing these things we are to be active in enforcing and feeding our faith, as well as acting on the Word of God and praising Him in advance for what He has already done. We are to have an attitude of thanksgiving at all times and a heart full of joy and expectation. The reason that this is labor is because often we do not feel like doing it. When battles are raging all around us and our mind and emotions are under siege by negative circumstances and challenges, we can begin to fall from the grace of God back into self-effort. Our feelings can begin to lead us away from the things we need to do to maintain our stance of faith in the finished works of Jesus. This is when we need to purpose to labor even more and become more intense in pushing back against the suggestions of the enemy. Verbally confessing the Word of God during times of adversity is labor, because it is difficult to do when we are experiencing issues. The same is true for praising God and offering up worship to Him when we don't feel like it. When we sacrifice our feelings in favor of speaking the Word of God and keeping our minds focused on Him, we are doing the work necessary to enter into and remain in a place of rest in Him.

## RELY ON THE SCRIPTURES

The Word of God is our foundation and the solid rock upon which we stand as believers. It is important to remember that our faith in what the Scriptures tell us about trust is what connects us to God's peace. First Peter 5:7 says to cast all your cares on God because He cares for you. This applies to all situations that we face. We were not designed by God to handle stress and worry. In fact, these things are counterproductive to the way God created us. They work to undermine our faith and rest in Him. Trusting God means refusing to be full of care about *anything*. Instead, *"in every thing by prayer and supplication with thanksgiving let your requests be made known unto God"* (Philippians 4:6). As believers, we must train ourselves to think this way. God loves to work when we rest. The greatest expression of faith in Him is to rest in His finished works. There is no place for worry, depression, fear, or doubt in the mind of a believer. We must push back against it with everything in us.

The story of Jesus feeding the five thousand is a great example of what it means to rest in the provision of God, even when things look impossible. When Jesus fed the crowd, He told the disciples to instruct the people to recline (John 6:10, *AMPC*). When you are reclining, you are in a resting position. If we follow what Jesus is doing here, it becomes clear that before we see manifestations, we must first rest. God promises to keep in perfect peace those whose minds are stayed on Him because they trust in Him (Isaiah 26:3). This is the key to beating stress and finding the peace of God no matter what is going on around you.

The Gospel is always being preached to all people, but the Word does not profit those who do not hear it in faith and rest in what grace has secured (Hebrews 4:2). In addition, those who do not believe in the finished works of Jesus will not put the Gospel in a position of priority, nor will they value it. Faith and a commitment to rest in what Jesus has accomplished are the keys to seeing the promises of God come to fruition in your life. Trust God, thank Him for what He has done, recline, take up a position of rest, and *expect* Him to deliver on His promises every single time. Your inheritance as a believer includes everything that God did before the foundation of the world. Simply believe you receive it and trust that what God has promised will come to pass!

# STUDY QUESTIONS

1. True or False: We can have confidence in ourselves, to an extent, when it comes to receiving God's finished works.

2. How can we develop our trust in God and be ready when trouble comes? ________

3. God wants us to trust Him enough to ________.

4. Why do we need God's guidance? ________

5. True or False: Our labor is required to receive God's promises.

6. What are some actions involved with resting in God? ________

7. Why is maintaining a faith stance in the midst of adversity difficult? __________

__________________________________________________

__________________________________________________

__________________________________________________

8. Our faith in what the Scriptures say about trust connects us to _______________

______________________________.

9. True or False: It is okay to worry a little bit about situations in life.

10. The greatest expression of faith in God is to ________________________.

# ANSWER KEY

1. False
2. by developing our faith in smaller things every day
3. rest in His promises
4. because we don't know what will happen tomorrow
5. False
6. standing in faith, speaking the Word, maintaining a position of trust
7. because it challenges the way we feel at the moment
8. God's peace
9. False
10. rest

**SCRIPTURE REFERENCES**

James 4:14, 15

Hebrews 4:1, 2, 11

Joshua 24:13

Deuteronomy 6:10-13

1 Peter 5:7

Philippians 4:6

John 6:10, *AMPC*

Isaiah 26:3

# CHAPTER TWENTY-SIX
# REST: THE KEY TO MANIFESTATION

The concept of rest for the Christian is often one that is sorely overlooked and not understood, and yet it is one of our most important instructions from God. Resting in the finished works of Jesus is the key to seeing the promises of God come to fruition in your life. Those who are born again are now under the covenant of grace and, under this new covenant, we find our rest in Jesus, who *is* the Word of God. We can say we are resting in Him, but this is only true if we find confidence in and rely on the Word of God and every one of its promises. We must recognize Jesus is both a person in the New Testament and the Word in the Old Testament. He is the culmination of it all! The only way to build our faith and remain in a posture of rest is to hear the Word of God on a consistent basis. In building our faith and renewing our mind to the finished works of Christ, we can live the abundant life that rightfully belongs to us as sons and daughters of God.

Walking by faith is not some kind of religious cliché; it is the lifestyle of the Christian. It is imperative that we understand all aspects of what it means to walk by faith if we are going to reap the benefits of it. The ultimate indicator of our faith in God and what He has said in His Word is actually rest. When we are not resting, we are demonstrating unbelief. The works of faith that God requires of us involve believing and trusting in Him fully. In order to do this, we must allow the Word to be our anchor in every area of life, all the time. Resting in Jesus essentially means resting in the Word of God. It means taking the Word of God and meditating on it until it becomes more real than the circumstance or situation. This is what produces unwavering trust. The truth is that you can't say you're resting in Jesus and not resting in the Word because Jesus and the Word are one and the same. You can't even properly relate to Jesus without spending time in the Bible. There simply must be a commitment to get in the Word of God and become intimate with it in order for resting in Jesus to become a reality in your life.

Hebrews 4:11 says, *"Let us labour therefore to enter into that rest, lest any man fall after the same example of unbelief."* God has already given us everything we need to succeed and thrive. For us, this means we do not need to labor to get rich, be healthy, get delivered, or to get anything else we want in life. We don't have to wrack our brains trying to figure out how to get what we desire and need to manifest. We must simply labor to reach the point where we have full confidence in what Jesus has done for us. Find the promise in the Word of God and refuse to come off the promise. It means resisting anything that presents itself to our senses as contrary information. This labor the Bible talks about is the concerted effort that we are to make to push past the distractions of the circumstances we face and maintain our peace no matter what. It is the peace that comes from keeping our undivided attention on Jesus, His Word, and what He has already accomplished for us. When we do that, we end up praising and thanking Him for it in advance.

Now, please understand that rest does not mean inactivity or an idle lifestyle. It is not resting *from* work, it is resting *in* work—the finished work of Jesus. While we are working or going about our normal day-to-day lives, we are to have such confidence and reliance on the Word that we are at peace, knowing that all our needs are met. While you are doing your job, you are resting in the financial increase that is coming from God. When you are exercising and eating healthy foods, you are resting in the divine health that belongs to you as a child of God. *"That the communication of thy faith may become effectual by the acknowledging of every good thing which is in you in*

*Christ Jesus"* (Philemon 1:6). When you are resting, you are still doing what God has told you to do every day to carry out your natural responsibilities, but you are believing in the supernatural power of God that is being released on your behalf through your faith in God's Word. Real proof that you are resting in the Word is when you can refer to specific Scriptures and apply them to your current situation.

## WALKING IN THE REST OF GOD

Religion teaches that you have to do something, and do it really hard, to get something from God. Many Christians have a hard time believing they can get something from God without having to labor for it, but everything pertaining to life and godliness has already been done (2 Peter 1:3). However, you must rest and have confidence in this truth.

A critical aspect of walking in the rest of God is to give Him all of our cares. This is particularly challenging to many believers, but it is what God requires of us. We can't access what He has done if we are holding on to what He has already taken care of! *"Humble yourselves therefore under the mighty hand of God, that he may exalt you in due time: Casting all your care upon him; for he careth for you"* (1 Peter 5:6, 7). God wants us to give Him what we are struggling to carry ourselves because we were never designed to carry the weights and burdens of this life. When we cast our cares on Him, we demonstrate true humility. When we carry worry, stress, and care, we are actually walking in pride. Real humility is submitting to the Word of God. *"Be careful for nothing; but in every thing by prayer and supplication with thanksgiving let your requests be made known unto God. And the peace of God, which passeth all understanding, shall keep your hearts and minds through Christ Jesus"* (Philippians 4:6, 7).

Jesus pointed out to the people that worry and anxiety would not add anything to their lives (Matthew 6:26, 27; Luke 12:24 26). Worry is negative meditation and it is one of the most toxic practices a believer can take part in on a daily basis. Worry prevents miracles and manifestations of God's Word from coming to pass. However, when you let go and let God, He will bless you generously and superabundantly. When you worry, you don't accomplish anything positive. Resting in the finished works of Jesus ensures God's blessings begin to flow into your life.

A powerful example of resting in the finished works of God is found in Second Chronicles 20. In this passage of Scripture, Jehoshaphat admitted to God that His people were outnumbered by their enemies and no one knew what to do, but that everyone's eyes were on Him. God told them to stand still and not fear, that the battle was His and not theirs. *"And when they began to sing and to praise, the Lord set ambushments against the children of Ammon, Moab, and mount Seir, which were come against Judah; and they were smitten"* (2 Chronicles 20:22). When the people entered into praise, God slew their enemies. *"And when Jehoshaphat and his people came to take away the spoil of them, they found among them in abundance both riches with the dead bodies, and precious jewels, which they stripped off for themselves, more than they could carry away: and they were three days in gathering of the spoil, it was so much"* (2 Chronicles 20:25).

Like Jehoshaphat and his people, we also face a battle every day, but this one is mental and psychological. It is a battle for control over our focus, and it is centered around getting us to turn away from what God has already done for us. But this is a battle that you can easily win by remaining steadfast in what God has promised in His Word. Satan can't directly impact your life without you giving him a platform of fear. When you do not know what to do, you must look at Jesus. This is His battle, not yours. Your job is simply to be still and know that He is God (Psalm 46:10). It is when you do this that you will see His deliverance come through for you. Enter into God's rest by maintaining unwavering confidence in Jesus, knowing that your trust in His finished works is what gives you access to the manifestation you are believing for.

# STUDY QUESTIONS

1. As covenant people, where do we find our rest? ____________________

2. True or False: Jesus is the Word of God.

3. How does faith come? ____________________

4. The works of faith God requires involve ____________________.

5. What does it mean to labor to enter into the rest of God? ____________________

6. True or False: It is okay to worry sometimes.

7. Releasing our cares to God demonstrates ________________________.

8. How are we to bring our requests to God? ________________________

________________________________________

________________________________________

________________________________________

9. What is a consequence of worry? ________________________

________________________________________

________________________________________

________________________________________

10. What is the main battle that we face as believers? ________________

________________________________________

________________________________________

________________________________________

# ANSWER KEY

1. in Jesus
2. True
3. by hearing the Word of God
4. believing and trusting in Him fully
5. making a concerted effort to push past the distractions of the circumstances we face and maintain our peace by keeping our undivided attention on Jesus, His Word, and what He has already accomplished for us
6. False
7. humility
8. with prayer and thanksgiving
9. It prevents miracles and manifestations from happening in our lives.
10. the battle for our focus

**SCRIPTURE REFERENCES**

Hebrews 4:11

Philemon 1:6

2 Peter 1:3

1 Peter 5:6, 7

Philippians 4:6, 7

Matthew 6:26, 27

Luke 12:24-26

2 Chronicles 20:22, 25

Psalm 46:10

# CHAPTER TWENTY-SEVEN
# RESTING IN THE FINISHED WORKS OF JESUS

There is a way to know if you are truly trusting God. It is directly connected to the extent that you find yourself resting in His finished works. In fact, there is no authentic belief in what God has said and done where there is worry, doubt, fear, or a general sense of unrest. If you find yourself being overcome by these emotions, it is time to take inventory of your faith and evaluate whether you are truly trusting God. Unbelief will rob you of the finished works of Jesus and keep you from ever seeing the manifestation of His promises in your life. We often try to get God to do things in our lives when those things have actually already been done. We get into self-effort because we don't realize or remember that grace has secured the blessing. The only way for God to work on your behalf is for you to rest. It is the greatest expression of your faith in Him. When you know without a shadow of a doubt that God's Word is true, panic cannot move you and you can see your faith through to fruition.

The key to entering into God's rest is to receive the finished works of Jesus Christ. This place is a place of confidence and trust, where we can experience the manifestations of what Jesus did two thousand years ago. Reaching this place hinges not on a life of laziness or inactivity, but on our strong faith in what God tells us in His Word. The Word is the blueprint and foundation for the promises that He has made to us. If we don't study and meditate on those promises, we won't have the faith to lay hold of them. Doubt prevents us from entering into His rest, and fear is a component of doubt. Fear tolerated is faith contaminated, which is why we must not be afraid to rely on Him, exclusively.

Hebrews 4:1-11 says:

> Let us therefore fear, lest, a promise being left us of entering into his rest, any of you should seem to come short of it. For unto us was the gospel preached, as well as unto them: but the word preached did not profit them, not being mixed with faith in them that heard it. For we which have believed do enter into rest, as he said, As I have sworn in my wrath, if they shall enter into my rest: although the works were finished from the foundation of the world. For he spake in a certain place of the seventh day on this wise, And God did rest the seventh day from all his works. And in this place again, If they shall enter into my rest. Seeing therefore it remaineth that some must enter therein, and they to whom it was first preached entered not in because of unbelief: Again, he limiteth a certain day, saying in David, To day, after so long a time; as it is said, To day if ye will hear his voice, harden not your hearts. For if Jesus had given them rest, then would he not afterward have spoken of another day. There remaineth therefore a rest to the people of God. For he that is entered into his rest, he also hath ceased from his own works, as God did from his. Let us labour therefore to enter into that rest, lest any man fall after the same example of unbelief.

Entering into God's rest and laboring to do so is of utmost importance. The Scripture lets us know that we should be vigilant and alert so that we do not come short of entering into God's rest; it is that important. Entering into His rest means that we cease from our own labors and completely rely on Jesus for everything we need or desire. While most people view resting as ceasing from all physical labor, it really means completely relying on Him while we go about our daily responsibilities, including working. We are not supposed to fold up, stop doing the things we need to do in this life, and wait for

God to move. We are in spiritual warfare on a daily basis, but Jesus has already won the battle. We are now to maintain that victory that He died to obtain. Operating in rest does not mean working for the victory, but working from a position of already having secured it. Under the Law of Moses, people worked for God; but under grace, He does amazing things for us when we rest.

In order to truly rest in the finished works of Jesus, we have to understand what He actually did for us. When He went to the cross, He took every punishment that we should have received so that we wouldn't have to. *"But he was wounded for our transgressions, he was bruised for our iniquities: the chastisement of our peace was upon him; and with his stripes we are healed"* (Isaiah 53:5). The wording of this Scripture is significant in that we see that healing comes after we receive His peace. This is significant because it gives us a picture of the truth that peace and rest precede manifestation of what God promised.

The story of Jesus feeding the multitude is a perfect example of how rest comes before the miraculous. *"Jesus said, Make all the people recline (sit down). Now the ground (a pasture) was covered with thick grass at the spot, so the men threw themselves down, about 5,000 in number. Jesus took the loaves, and when He had given thanks, He distributed to the disciples and the disciples to the reclining people; so also [He did] with the fish, as much as they wanted"* (John 6:10, 11, *AMPC*). This biblical account tells of an amazing miracle that demonstrates how we must be at rest to partake of the supernatural. Jesus had the people sit down, first, before they were fed. He made sure they were in a posture of relaxation *before* they received from Him. They ate their fill only after they had reclined. So likewise, we must be at rest to partake of miracles. When we learn to recline in God, sitting back and trusting that He provides, we will see God's multiplication take place.

Maintaining a mind that is anchored on God and His Word is the key to perfect peace. In fact, God promises to keep in perfect peace those whose minds are focused on Him. The reason a person's mind can remain focused on Him is because they trust in Him (Isaiah 26:3). When we focus on the Word of God, we are focusing on Jesus, Himself. As a result, we will have peace and security in the midst of turmoil.

So, how do you keep your mind focused on God? You do it by finding Scriptures that cover the particular area or issue you are facing and standing on them no matter what. This takes a commitment to aggressively push back against any and all attacks against your senses to draw you away from your focus on the finished works. When thoughts come to move you, that is when you open your mouth and declare the promise. In this way, you maintain your position of rest and enforce the victory over the circumstance.

Believing God is working with you, in you, and for you is another key to remaining confident. The children of Israel didn't believe and they ended up wandering in the wilderness for forty years. God's perspective is always, "Why don't they believe Me?" Hope comes from the things that are written in the Word, whether in the Old Testament or the New, which is why God allowed His words to be transcribed for our reference today (Romans 15:4). While man wrote the Bible, it was inspired by God so we can rest assured that it is true and that we can rely on it at all times (2 Timothy 3:16). The Word is infallible proof of God's love, mercy, grace, and commitment to mankind. We can rest in it with complete assurance.

Whether under the Law of Moses or under grace, throughout the Scriptures we learn of the importance of God's rest. Although we are no longer under the law, the law is still part of God's Word and we can take principles from it for our reference today. The concept of the Sabbath was a high priority under the law and we can glean valuable insight from it. God rested from His labors on the seventh day. He blessed the seventh day because it was a day of rest (Genesis 2:2, 3). God didn't rest because He was tired; He rested because His work was finished and it was perfect. We cannot ever work hard enough to outdo what God has done. He has set the system up so that He gets all the credit and the glory from the manifestation of His promises. We cannot boast about the hand that we had in them (John 15:5). Just as the Sabbath was to represent God resting from His work on the seventh day, Jesus is our rest from work today. Jesus is our Sabbath. He is our place of rest and our refuge from self-effort. When we put our trust in Jesus, we demonstrate that we are relying on Him and Him, alone, for everything pertaining to our lives.

The person who knows that all of God's works are already completed never walks in fear or panic. *"Because thou hast been my help, therefore in the shadow of thy wings will I rejoice"* (Psalm 63:7). God wants us to be aware that we need His help and that, apart from Him, we can do nothing. *"I can do all things* ***through Christ*** *which strengtheneth me"* (Philippians 4:13, emphasis mine). He tells us not to fear because He will save us, but we must rest and be at ease (Jeremiah 46:27). It is up to us to labor to enter into the rest that God wants us to experience. Praise, worship, and thanksgiving are ways to magnify God in our minds and keep our focus on Him. Our position of rest sends a message to the spiritual realm that we are in full receiving-mode. God fulfills His Word for those who believe in what He has already done.

# STUDY QUESTIONS

1. True or False: Wherever there is no rest, there is no authentic belief in what God has said.

2. ______________________ will rob you of the finished works of Jesus.

3. ______________________ is the only way for God to work on your behalf.

4. How do we enter into God's rest? ______________________

______________________

______________________

______________________

5. How do we get to a place of confidence? ______________________

______________________

______________________

______________________

6. What is our job in spiritual warfare? ______________________

______________________

______________________

______________________

7. What must precede manifestation? ______________________________

8. How do you keep your mind focused on Jesus? ______________________________

9. True or False: The Sabbath was a high priority in the law.

10. Why did God rest? ______________________________

# ANSWER KEY

1. True
2. Unbelief
3. Resting
4. by receiving all the finished works of Jesus Christ
5. through our strong faith in what God tells us in His Word
6. to maintain the position of victory Jesus has secured
7. peace
8. by finding the Scriptures that cover the particular issue you're facing and standing on them
9. True
10. because His work was finished

**SCRIPTURE REFERENCES**

Hebrews 4:1-11

Isaiah 53:5

John 6:10, 11, *AMPC*

Isaiah 26:3

Romans 15:4

2 Timothy 3:16

Genesis 2:2, 3

John 15:5

Psalm 63:7

Philippians 4:13

Jeremiah 46:27

# CHAPTER TWENTY-EIGHT
# LET GOD WORK FOR YOU

Salvation is more than just "fire insurance" or being rescued from hell after you die. It actually encompasses all of the finished works of Jesus Christ. That means your deliverance, healing, prosperity, and everything pertaining to life and godliness are wrapped up in salvation. When Jesus shed His blood, He made all of these wonderful things available to every human being on the planet, but every person is not walking in or experiencing the benefits of salvation. Why is that? Simply put, it is because they have not taken possession of what belongs to them. God wants us to experience every single promise found in His Word, and there is nothing we have to do to earn these promises. That may sound like a far-fetched concept, especially when we are conditioned to believe that we have to work to get Him to do something for us, but the truth is that the finished works of Jesus Christ have already been completed. For the person who is not saved, the first step is to receive Jesus as Lord and Savior. After that, we must renew our minds and then labor to enter into the rest of God. It is the same rest that God entered into when He finished His work on the seventh day. This rest is the eternal Sabbath that is represented through Jesus Christ's finished work. It is the resting place that releases the actual manifestation of those works. When we maintain rest, we can see continual blessings in our lives.

As Christians, we already know that grace has made available everything necessary for a successful life. In fact, the grace of God is all you will ever need. *"Blessed be the God and Father of our Lord Jesus Christ, who hath blessed us with all spiritual blessings in heavenly places in Christ"* (Ephesians 1:3). Healing, financial provision, deliverance, and more are available to us at any moment. When Jesus said, "It is finished" just before He died on the cross, all of God's promises to us were cemented into place. Sometimes, believers make the mistake of trying to do something that is already completed when all God wants us to do is simply believe, have faith, and rest in what He did. The challenge lies in determining what we should do to see the manifestations of what has already been done. The main thing that we must do constantly is renew our minds with the Word of God and allow it to be our final authority on all matters. Remember that renewing your mind is a lifetime process that should take place on an ongoing basis. When you constantly renew your mind with the Word of God, you allow it to change the way you think. When your thinking begins to line up with the way God sees things, you will see manifestations begin to take place in your life.

When we rest in Jesus, God begins to carry out what we have faith for. We don't have to do anything to get Him to move on our behalf. *"Let us therefore fear, lest, a promise being left us of entering into his rest, any of you should seem to come short of it. For unto us was the gospel preached, as well as unto them: but the word preached did not profit them, not being mixed with faith in them that heard it"* (Hebrews 4:1, 2). While the Gospel of Jesus Christ has been preached to many people, only those who mix faith with hearing the Word will see it come to pass in their lives. When we rest, we demonstrate that we have faith that is immovable. The promises of God are available to all people, but not everyone will experience these promises because they won't take possession of them. The evidence of taking possession is an unwavering position of rest, no matter what things look like.

The reason God wants us to rely on His finished works is because that allows Him to get the credit for the results instead of us. When we do something in our own ability, we can boast about it; but when God does something, He gets all the glory (Romans 4:1, 2). We are not saved because of our goodness, but because of His goodness toward us.

The biblical accounts of the woman with the issue of blood and Jairus' daughter being raised to life are two wonderful examples of the supernatural results that can take place when someone believes in Jesus, focuses on Him with unwavering intent, and rests in His ability. In Mark 5, we see Jesus' ministry in action as He steps off the ship in which He was traveling.

> And when Jesus was passed over again by ship unto the other side, much people gathered unto him: and he was nigh unto the sea. And, behold, there cometh one of the rulers of the synagogue, Jairus by name; and when he saw him, he fell at his feet, And besought him greatly, saying, My little daughter lieth at the point of death: I pray thee, come and lay thy hands on her, that she may be healed; and she shall live. And Jesus went with him; and much people followed him, and thronged him. And a certain woman, which had an issue of blood twelve years, And had suffered many things of many physicians, and had spent all that she had, and was nothing bettered, but rather grew worse, When she had heard of Jesus, came in the press behind, and touched his garment. For she said, If I may touch but his clothes, I shall be whole. And straightway the fountain of her blood was dried up; and she felt in her body that she was healed of that plague...And he said unto her, Daughter, thy faith hath made thee whole; go in peace, and be whole of thy plague (Mark 5:21-29, 34).

This woman had an issue that was incurable by natural means. Nothing she had tried worked, but when she encountered Jesus, she came in contact with the only power that could heal her. She risked it all to have a chance at touching Him because the infirmity she had prevented her, by law, from being out in public. She had that much faith and that much focus on the anointing that Jesus possessed that she took a chance with her life, just to touch the hem of His garment. She was immediately healed of that infirmity that had plagued her all those years. Jesus told her that her faith was what made her whole.

> While he yet spake, there came from the ruler of the synagogue's house certain which said, Thy daughter is dead: why troublest thou the Master any further? As soon as Jesus heard the word that was spoken, he saith unto the ruler of the synagogue, Be not afraid, only believe. And he suffered no man to follow him, save Peter, and James, and John the brother of James. And he cometh to the house of the ruler of the synagogue, and seeth the tumult, and them that wept and wailed greatly. And when he was come in, he saith unto them, Why make ye this ado, and weep? the damsel is not dead, but sleepeth. And they laughed him to scorn. But when he had put them all out, he taketh the father and the mother of the damsel, and them that were with him, and entereth in where the damsel was lying. And he took the damsel by the hand, and said unto her, Talitha cumi; which is, being interpreted, Damsel, I say unto thee, arise. And straightway the damsel arose, and walked; for she was of the age of twelve years. And they were astonished with a great astonishment (Mark 5:35-42).

When Jesus raised this little girl from the dead, He told her father to not have fear, but only believe. Needless to say, the miraculous power of God showed up once again, and this man's daughter was resurrected.

What is the common denominator between these two accounts? In both cases, faith was released and the individuals rested in what they believed Jesus would do. They had that level of trust and rest *before* their manifestation happened! Believers must take the same position. Grace is available to everyone, but faith is required to take possession of what grace has secured. When we release our faith in the finished works of Jesus, we will get the same kind of miraculous results that these people did thousands of years ago. What Jairus and the woman with the issue of blood displayed was a high level of faith. Both of these people came to Jesus because they had heard of Him and believed in His ability to heal their situations. The woman did not receive healing simply by hearing about it; she had to act in faith to take possession of it. When Jesus told Jairus not to fear but to believe, His intention was to keep Jairus at rest so that fear would not hinder his faith.

Grace makes the promises of God available, but faith takes those promises and lays hold of them. Just like those two individuals, we must focus on the Word of God (Jesus) and act in faith by doing whatever the Lord instructs for our situation. Our faith released through a practical expression of our confidence in God and His Word combined with absolute confidence in what Jesus has done for us allows us to take possession of His finished works right now. In doing so, the power of God goes to work on our behalf and we are able to actually experience supernatural results. When this happens, we demonstrate to the world who God is and that His grace is sufficient to meet every need we have. Let God do the work for you by resting in His promises!

# STUDY QUESTIONS

1. True or False: The believer must earn God's promises.

2. What is the believer's "work"? ______

3. What is the significance of the Sabbath? ______

4. What was the significance of Jesus saying, "It is finished"? ______

5. How do we see the manifestations of what has already been done? ______

6. When we rest, we are demonstrating that we have ____________________ and that it is ____________________.

7. Only those who mix ____________________ with hearing the Word will see it come to pass.

8. Why does God want us to rely only on His finished works? ____________________

____________________

____________________

____________________

9. True or False: Our goodness plays a role in our salvation.

10. What makes the promises of God available? ____________________

____________________

____________________

____________________

# ANSWER KEY

1. False
2. the labor of entering into the rest of God
3. It represents the eternal finished works of Christ.
4. It cemented all of God's promises into place.
5. by constantly renewing our minds with the Word of God
6. faith; immovable
7. faith
8. so that only He gets the credit
9. False
10. grace

**SCRIPTURE REFERENCES**

Ephesians 1:3

Hebrews 4:1, 2

Romans 4:1, 2

Mark 5:21-29, 34-42

# CHAPTER TWENTY-NINE
# THE PRACTICAL SIDE OF REST

As Christians, it is one thing to talk about resting in God, and another thing to know how to actually enter into that rest. Working our faith is a key component, because when we keep our faith working until we have peace, we reach that point of rest. The devil does not want us to rest or be at peace. One of his strategies is to move us from our place of rest by instilling fear into us and suggesting that the promises made in the Word of God will not come to pass; but we must remember that fear tolerated is faith contaminated. God needs our faith in order to bring us the manifestations we seek. Studying the Scriptures, we find some useful tools we can use while working to rest.

Remember that the Word of God only works if it is mixed with our faith. "*For unto us was the gospel preached, as well as unto them: but the word preached did not profit them, not being mixed with faith in them that heard it. For we which have believed do enter into rest, as he said, As I have sworn in my wrath, if they shall enter into my rest: although the works were finished from the foundation of the world... Let us labour therefore to enter into that rest, lest any man fall after the same example of unbelief*" (Hebrews 4:2, 3, 11). The Scripture lets us know that those who did not hear the Gospel in faith didn't benefit from it. We also see here that if we want to see the manifestation of the finished works of Jesus, we must first enter into that place of rest.

So, what does it mean to rest? It means to have confidence, trust, and reliance on God. It means that we cast our cares over on Him, knowing that He cares for us and that we were not created to carry worry, stress, anxiety, or the cares of this life. In fact, these negative things will actually block any manifestations that we want to see in our lives. What we seek will only manifest itself when we reach the place of rest. It is in this place that we will access the peace that precedes manifestation.

As you go through life, there will be times that you are emotionally shaken by circumstances; but in the midst of those times, there are some practical steps you can take to find your place of rest. First, you need to find the specific Scripture that refers to your situation. This Scripture will be your anchor of peace. Isaiah 26:3 says that the person who keeps his or her mind stayed on Jesus will be kept in perfect peace. John 14:27 speaks about the peace that Jesus leaves us, a peace that can't be taken away by the world: *"Peace I leave with you, my peace I give unto you: not as the world giveth, give I unto you. Let not your heart be troubled, neither let it be afraid."* You must have an anchor Scripture that you hold on to in the midst of your storm. It is the Scripture that will enable you to walk through the challenge with peace and confidence.

Second, you need to meditate on the answer found in the Word of God. Keep meditating on it until you can see it in your imagination. Proverbs 23:7 says, *"For as he thinketh in his heart, so is he."* Continual meditation is what renews your mind and gets the solution deeply embedded in your consciousness. *"This book of the law shall not depart out of thy mouth; but thou shalt meditate therein day and night, that thou mayest observe to do according to all that is written therein: for then thou shalt make thy way prosperous, and then thou shalt have good success"* (Joshua 1:8). When you meditate on Scripture, you ponder it, think about it, and turn it over in your mind again and again so that you can get all the revelation you can out of it. The more you meditate on the Word of God, the more faith will begin to rise within you and you will find yourself maintaining a position of peace.

The third step is to let what you say agree with what you believe. Romans 4:17 says,

*"As it is written, I have made thee a father of many nations, before him whom he believed, even God, who quickeneth the dead, and calleth those things which be not as though they were."* Agreement between your words and your beliefs is critical to seeing the finished works of Jesus become a reality in your everyday life. You can't say you believe what God has done and then speak words that are contrary to that belief. In doing so, you cancel your faith and delay the promise from coming to pass. Your words and beliefs must align for maximum agreement. Only speak the Word of God; only declare the promise. Words that agree with your faith release God's creative ability into the earth.

The fourth step to finding your place of rest is to begin thanking and praising God for what you found in the Scriptures. Praise and thanksgiving are powerful tools in your faith arsenal. Gratitude and outward expressions of praise and thanks to God invite Him on the scene and paralyze the devil. Stay in continual praise and watch what happens!

Finally, pray in tongues! Praying in tongues is the believer's most important prayer tool for several reasons. First, when you pray in tongues, you are praying directly to God. *"For one who speaks in an [unknown] tongue speaks not to men but to God, for no one understands or catches his meaning, because in the [Holy] Spirit he utters secret truths and hidden things [not obvious to the understanding]"* (1 Corinthians 14:2, *AMPC*). Your own understanding and agenda are not involved, which means that you are praying the perfect prayer. A prayer in tongues allows the Holy Spirit to pray through you and it releases Him to get involved in your situation without your interference. Praying in tongues also edifies your spirit and heals those areas of your soul that need to be restored. It strengthens you where you are weak and releases most holy faith, the highest kind of faith possible. *"But you, beloved, build yourselves up [founded] on your most holy faith [make progress, rise like an edifice higher and higher], praying in the Holy Spirit"* (Jude 1:20, *AMPC*). Praying in tongues releases an immediate sense of peace in your spirit, soul, and body. It is a supernatural type of prayer.

Keep in mind that the personal prayer language of the believer, praying in tongues, is not the same as the gift of the spirit of tongues. The *spirit of tongues* typically goes forth in a corporate setting and requires the gift of interpretation so that the hearers of the prophetic word that was released in tongues can understand what God was saying. The *prayer language of tongues* is part of the baptism of the Holy Spirit and is available to every Christian who receives it (Isaiah 28:11, 12; Romans 8:26; 1 Corinthians 14:14). It is a powerful way to communicate with God and get Him involved with your situation.

### CREATED TO REST

God created mankind to rest. We can see reminders of this all around us. The rest referred to in the Old Testament is a precursor of the New Testament and the finished works of Christ that are now available to us. The Sabbath is not just a 24-hour period of time; it is actually Jesus, Himself. He is our Sabbath, our ultimate rest and place of peace.

God blessed the seventh day because it was then when He rested from all His work (Genesis 2:3). The people were instructed to remember the Sabbath day and keep it holy (Exodus 20:8-11). This aspect of the Law of Moses was a type and shadow of the rest that Jesus would make available to us through His sacrifice on the cross. While we are not under the law, and therefore observance of a 24-hour period is not something we have to do as Christians (Colossians 2:16, 17), the Sabbath concept is something that we should continually live. It is the posture that stays in a "reclined" position of peace and rest, in confident expectation of the manifestation of God's finished works in our lives coming to pass.

We can take a look at nature and see the creation of God resting and receiving from the Father. For example, the birds and the flowers do not work, yet they are provided for (Matthew 6:26-29). We are much more valuable than they are, so if God takes care of them with such ease, how much more will He take care of us? We don't have to worry and fret, but follow the example of God's other creations and simply relax in His provisions for us.

Since Jesus is our rest, He teaches us how to handle trouble and adversity. When Jesus got into a boat with His disciples and a storm overtook them, He was completely at rest (Mark 4:35-41). In fact, when Jesus was resting, He was actually controlling the storm. This man, Jesus, who was in the disciples' boat, is the same one who is in our boat when storms hit our lives. If we are in Him, we are also at rest in the midst of a storm.

*"Come unto me, all ye that labour and are heavy laden, and I will give you rest. Take my yoke upon you, and learn of me; for I am meek and lowly in heart: and ye shall find rest unto your souls"* (Matthew 11:28, 29). Jesus gives rest to their souls and He will give rest to yours. When you labor without God, all you get is a heavy burden (Psalm 127:1, 2). When you allow God to carry the weight of the things you are going through, you can move through life with ease, even when challenges come. Executing the practical steps to rest will help you go to the next level in your faith and keep you focused on the finished works of Jesus, which include every aspect of the abundant life.

# STUDY QUESTIONS

1. When will we reach the point of rest as Christians? ______

______

______

2. How does the devil try to move us from our place of peace? ______

______

______

______

3. Fear tolerated is ______ contaminated.

4. The Word of God only benefits you if it is mixed with ______.

5. What does it mean to rest? ______

______

6. What is the first step to finding your place of rest? ______

______

7. What does it mean to meditate on the Word? ____________________

______________________________________________

______________________________________________

______________________________________________

8. True or False: You can believe the Word and speak something different.

9. What are some benefits of praying in tongues? ____________________

______________________________________________

______________________________________________

______________________________________________

10. True or False: Today, the Sabbath is an actual 24-hour period.

# ANSWER KEY

1. when we keep our faith working until we get to the point of peace
2. by instilling a spirit of fear
3. faith
4. faith
5. to have confidence, trust, and reliance on God
6. find the specific Scripture that relates to your situation
7. to think about it, ponder it, and turn it over in your mind to get revelation from it
8. False
9. you pray the perfect prayer directly to God, your spirit is edified, you overcome your weaknesses
10. False

**SCRIPTURE REFERENCES**

Hebrews 4:2, 3, 11

Isaiah 26:3

John 14:27

Proverbs 23:7

Joshua 1:8

Romans 4:17

1 Corinthians 14:2, *AMPC*

Jude 1:20, *AMPC*

Isaiah 28:11, 12

Romans 8:26

1 Corinthians 14:14

Genesis 2:3

Exodus 20:8-11

Colossians 2:16, 17

Matthew 6:26-29

Mark 4:35-41

Matthew 11:28, 29

Psalm 127:1, 2

# CHAPTER THIRTY
# RESTING ON PURPOSE

What does it mean to enter into God's rest and why is it so important in the life of a believer? Resting in God means having absolute confidence and trust in what He has already done so that you are not trying to make His promises come to pass in your life through your own ability. Entering into God's rest is important for each and every one of us, but it is on an entirely voluntary basis—He will not force it on anyone. It hinges on our belief in what Jesus has done. This confidence empowers us to take on a "reclining" spiritual posture, even in the midst of circumstances and situations that challenge our faith. While the world is stressing out and worrying about things, the believer is at rest in the knowledge of God's love for them. Resting in God calms us, focuses us, and gives us peace while we go about our daily lives. Having this kind of peace allows us to prosper in whatever we do. Whatever it takes, we must reach this point of spiritual rest.

Hebrews 4:3 is the foundation for understanding what resting in God is all about. It says, *"For we which have believed do enter into rest."* Remember, rest does not mean inactivity or that you stop working at your job or take a permanent vacation from your responsibilities. It means that while you work you find rest in what God has accomplished. There are two types of works in the Bible: the works of the law (where you try to get God to do something through your own performance) and the works of faith (where you now receive, by faith, what Jesus has already done). There is a big difference between the two. Those who believe in the finished works of Jesus are resting and allowing their lives to reflect that rest with works of faith (practical expressions of their confidence in what Jesus has done). These are the ones who find peace and confidence in what is already done. When you are peaceful and at rest in Him, what you do will prosper.

If you want the perfect example of how to enter into God's rest by faith, look no further than Jesus, Himself. He provides the prototype of how to do this. You see, Jesus was able to do the things that He did and maintain the position that He did because of His connection to the Father. This rest of God is entered into by those who believe what God has said in His Word. When you are in Jesus Christ, you are connected to the Father and you have the assurance of His abundant supply in every area of your life. Rest is the by-product of an unwavering belief in God's Word. Jesus was completely human and He was tempted by sin, yet He never yielded to it (2 Corinthians 5:21). Romans 5:20 says that when sin abounds, grace abounds even more; but Jesus didn't sin and the grace of God was constantly increasing in His life (Luke 2:40). What was responsible for this abounding grace? It was His faith in what the Word had declared about Him. It produced complete rest and peace. Jesus was never stressed out, but remained in the rest of God.

Just like Jesus continually rested in the Father and His love, we can rest in Jesus because He was the ultimate sacrifice for our sins. A place of rest is a place of reliance and trust where you are leaning and depending totally on Him for everything. When you stay in the secret place of the Most High, the devil can't figure you out. He doesn't understand why you don't panic. This is the safest and most liberating place a Christian can be.

Jesus provides the most powerful example of rest for us to follow. He consistently remained at rest, even in the face of daunting situations like being in the midst of a storm while on a boat with His disciples (Mark 4:35-41), His enemies attempting to throw

Him off a cliff (Luke 4:28-30), and extreme persecution from the religious leaders of the day (Matthew 22:15-46; Mark 8:11-13; Luke 11:53, 54). Even in the garden of Gethsemane, He labored to enter into God's rest to the point of sweating blood (Luke 22:44). When He was called upon to raise people from the dead or heal the sick in the face of others' unbelief, He never flinched. His position of rest never changed.

As believers, we are only at rest if we cast our cares over on God and let Him work on our behalf. Hebrews 4:9 says that there remains a rest for God's people. We must choose to enter into this rest on purpose. Jesus came in contact with individuals who were sick and afflicted, who had struggled a long time trying to fix their own situations. When they finally gave up, rested from their own efforts, and accepted what Jesus offered them, He turned things around for them. He healed several people and performed miracles on the Sabbath, which is a day of rest (Luke 6:6-10; Luke 13:10-13; John 5:1-16). These biblical accounts—the man with the withered hand, the woman who was oppressed with a spirit of infirmity, and the paralyzed man at the pool of Bethesda—give us a picture of the deliverance, healing, and miracle-working power of God that is available to us when we choose to rest in Him and let go of trying to change our situations in our own ability.

God works in us to accomplish His will, and it is not of our own strength. In fact, nothing about our own strength can accomplish the plans of God in our lives. *"[Not in your own strength] for it is God Who is all the while effectually at work in you [energizing and creating in you the power and desire], both to will and to work for His good pleasure and satisfaction and delight"* (Philippians 2:13, *AMPC*). For example, we can't break a habit through the use of our own willpower. Trying to modify our behavior this way does not work. Changed behavior comes through changed beliefs. We must believe who we are in Christ and believe in the grace that has been made available to us to live in a way that pleases God. When we put our faith in Him and His finished works, we are infused with the empowerment to overcome the habits that hinder our progress.

Part of resting in God on purpose is making a conscious decision to be anxious for nothing. God did not create us to carry care or to live in stress. He wants us to give every worry and anxiety over to Him (1 Peter 5:7). This is an act of your will. Instead of taking on the care of life's challenges, take all of your requests to God in prayer and supplication, and His peace, which surpasses all understanding, will guard your heart and mind through Jesus (Philippians 4:6, 7). Make a quality decision to rest on purpose. Everything that we struggle with should be handed over to God, regardless of what the issue is. You can practice this by speaking the Word of God when thoughts try to intrude on your mind, praising God, and magnifying Him throughout the day. You will discover how quickly your focus shifts from the problem to the solution. When you enter into His rest on purpose, you release God to go to work on the situation and bring you through with flying colors. By choosing rest as a way of life, the blessings of God can flow effortlessly to us.

# STUDY QUESTIONS

1. True or False: Experiencing God's rest is a voluntary act of your will.

2. ______________________________ empowers us to rest even in the midst of our labors.

3. ______________________________ provides the prototype of how to rest.

4. Who enters the rest of God? ______________________________

______________________________

5. When you are in Christ, you have the assurance of ______________________________

______________________________.

6. Why can we rest in Jesus? ______________________________

______________________________

7 How do we know when we are resting in God's finished works? ______________________________

______________________________

8. How does true change come? ____________________________________________

____________________________________________

____________________________________________

____________________________________________

9. True or False: Carrying a little stress should be expected in the life of a believer.

# ANSWER KEY

1. True
2. Confidence in what God has done through Jesus
3. Jesus
4. those who believe what God has said in His Word
5. His abundant supply in every area of your life
6. because He was the ultimate sacrifice for our sins
7. when we cast all our cares on Him
8. by believing who we are in Christ and believing in the grace that has been made available to us to live in way that pleases God.
9. False

**SCRIPTURE REFERENCES**

Hebrews 4:3, 9

2 Corinthians 5:21

Romans 5:20

Luke 2:40

Mark 4:35-41

Luke 4:28-30

Matthew 22:15-46

Mark 8:11-13

Luke 11:53, 54

Luke 22:44

Luke 6:6-10

Luke 13:10-13

John 5:1-16

Philippians 2:13, *AMPC*

1 Peter 5:7

Philippians 4:6, 7, *AMPC*

# CHAPTER THIRTY-ONE
# THE POWER OF RESTING IN JESUS

Resting in God is one of the most vital subjects for Christians to get hold of because it is necessary in order to see the promises of God come to pass in your life. It is one thing to hear about resting in God, and it's another to know that you will be challenged in this area every day. The devil also knows how important this is and he will do everything he can to prevent us from entering our place of rest. He definitely will not roll out the red carpet and make resting in God easy, but if we can reach this point of absolute trust and rest in the promises of God, we will be able to find grace in a time of trouble, the solutions to our problems, and the manifestations of God that rightfully belong to us as believers. We must, however, let go of stress, worry, and everything that holds us back. This means choosing the supernatural over the superficial. When we do, we will find that we are no longer in a place of lack and despair, but in the land of abundance, where everything we need is readily available.

Hebrews 4:3 says that those who believe enter into God's rest, but what is it that we are resting on and what is it that we need to believe? We are resting in the truth of the finished works of Jesus, that what He did over two thousand years ago is a done deal.

If you believe that two thousand years ago your deliverance was completed, then that deliverance will manifest in your life. If you believe that your prosperity has already been taken care of, then prosperity will show up every day. Healing, deliverance, and success in every arena of life were taken care of when Jesus died on the cross. Believing these things is what activates the manifestation of them on a daily basis. You will never receive the benefits of your covenant if you don't believe them. If you don't believe that Jesus has already taken care of these things, you will never find rest in them.

Religion teaches us that we need to work to get God to do something, but faith in Jesus says, "It is already done," and takes it now. Resting in God isn't referring to inactivity or not doing anything and just expecting things to magically happen. No, resting is finding peace and confidence while working and moving through life. It is doing what you have to do without the stress, care, and worry that accompany those who don't know Jesus Christ. We are to work out of a position of rest, which means we believe God. This enables us to be empowered in what we are doing. When trials and tribulations come in life, we are not flustered because we know God loves us. When you are peaceful and at rest in Jesus, you will have success in the things you are doing. Peace is security in the midst of a storm, and it is the character of Christ which we possess.

Keep in mind that the grace of God does not just abound because sin is present. The Scriptures say that Jesus abounded in grace even as a child (Luke 2:40). We know that Jesus never sinned (2 Corinthians 5:21), so the grace that was on His life had nothing to do with Him missing the mark. While it is true that grace abounds when sin is present (Romans 5:20), grace can be on your life for another reason. This reason is what every believer needs to get hold of.

In Genesis 6:8, we find the word "grace" being used for the first time: *"But Noah found grace in the eyes of the Lord."* This is significant because the name Noah means rest. If we plug the word rest into this Scripture, it reads, "Rest found grace in the eyes of the Lord." What a powerful revelation! When you rest, that's when you will find the grace that will help you in the time of need. You won't find grace when you're worried, stressed out, and full of care. Only when you rest will you find grace. Jesus, Himself, always rested in the Father. In John 5:19, Jesus said that He could do nothing apart from what He saw the Father doing. So likewise, there is a rest that remains for God's people (Hebrews 4:9).

Evidence of the power of resting in the finished works of Jesus can be seen in many of the healings and miracles that He performed. Three in particular are significant as it relates to rest: the man with a withered hand, the woman who was oppressed with a spirit of infirmity, and the paralyzed man at the pool of Bethesda. These people received their miracles on the Sabbath, when they rested from their self-efforts (Luke 6:6-10; Luke 13:10-13; John 5:1-16). They were healed when they trusted Jesus.

Perhaps the reason that so many people are not receiving the manifestations they are believing for is because they are striving and working hard to get results, instead of simply resting in the finished works of Jesus. Letting go of the idea that you have to do something to make God move for you is the key to everything you are believing God for.

Jesus had absolute mastery over the circumstances that came to challenge His position of rest, and He remained confident in the Father's ability working through Him. John 5:19 says, "*Then answered Jesus and said unto them, Verily, verily, I say unto you, The Son can do nothing of himself, but what he seeth the Father do: for what things soever he doeth, these also doeth the Son likewise.*" Just as Jesus rested in the Father, we must also trust and rely completely on what Jesus has accomplished. Grace comes on you when you do this.

Hebrews 4:9 says, "*There remaineth therefore a rest to the people of God.*" How comforting! There is a rest for you today that is waiting for you to enter into and enjoy. Many times we are not seeing the hand of God moving in our lives because we've been taught by religion to worry, strive, and work. It is time for believers to stop trusting in their own ability to get something done and trust what God has already done.

God works in us to do His will, and it is in His strength, not our own, that we are energized to work for His delight. Philippians 2:13 emphasizes this. We can't do anything in our own ability, but God can give us the desire to do what pleases Him. For example, we are not strong enough through our willpower to break ingrained habits, but through Him we can. God takes away the temptation, and He gives us the desire and ability to stop doing those things that are not beneficial for us to do. Again, it is through resting in the finished works of Jesus that we can do this. The finished works include deliverance. By meditating on the Word of God and receiving the truth of this deliverance, our confidence in it develops, which gives us the ability to walk in the deliverance that belongs to us.

Philippians 4:6 encourages us to release our cares and, instead of worrying about things, go to God in prayer, with thanksgiving. When we do this, the peace of God will invade our lives and keep our minds and hearts stable through the power of Christ. *"But grow in grace, and in the knowledge of our Lord and Saviour Jesus Christ. To him be glory both now and for ever. Amen"* (2 Peter 3:18). Grace is multiplied when we maintain our peace (2 Peter 1:2). God wants you to experience more grace and more peace in your life, but you have to fill yourself with the knowledge of what Jesus has already done so that His grace and peace can rest on you.

Jesus has been made unto us wisdom, righteousness, sanctification, and redemption (1 Corinthians 1:30). When you really believe these things belong to you because He lives in you, you will have peace, no matter what happens in your life. You will know who you are and have confidence in your identity in Him, which will move you into a position of rest. This is why meditating on the Word of God is so vital.

Looking to God's grace to do what you can't do in your own ability is the whole premise of resting in Jesus. By focusing on rest rather than self-effort, you demonstrate that you need Him. God loves this because He wants to be involved in your life! When a bill shows up and you don't know where the money is coming from, don't panic. Start declaring the provision of God because of what Jesus has already done (Philippians 4:19). When the doctor gives you a bad medical report, instead of agreeing with him, you agree with the truth, which is that by His stripes you were healed (1 Peter 2:24). No circumstance can stand against the faith and trust of a believer who has chosen to rest (Matthew 11:28-30). Refuse to deviate from the finished works of Jesus and you will see true and lasting inward transformation in your life and circumstances.

# STUDY QUESTIONS

1. Why is resting in God one of the most vital subjects for Christians to master?

_______________________________________________

_______________________________________________

_______________________________________________

2. What keeps us from resting in Jesus' finished works? ________________

_______________________________________________

_______________________________________________

_______________________________________________

3. What is it that we rest on as believers? ________________

_______________________________________________

_______________________________________________

_______________________________________________

4 Resting in God is finding ________________________

and ________ ________________________ while going about your daily life.

5. True or False: The grace of God abounds only when sin is present.

6. Peace is ______________________________________.

7. When do you find grace to resolve your situation? ____________________

________________________________________________

8. Why are many Christians not receiving the manifestation of their faith? ________

________________________________________________

________________________________________________

________________________________________________

9. What is the premise of resting in Jesus? __________________________

________________________________________________

________________________________________________

# ANSWER KEY

1. because it is necessary for the promises of God to come to pass in your life
2. stress, worry, and anxiety
3. the finished works of Jesus
4. peace; confidence
5. False
6. security in the midst of a storm
7. when you rest
8. because they are striving and working hard to get results instead of resting in the finished works
9. looking to God's grace to do what you can't do in your own ability

## SCRIPTURE REFERENCES

Hebrews 4:3

Luke 2:40

2 Corinthians 5:21

Romans 5:20

Genesis 6:8

John 5:19

Hebrews 4:9

Luke 6:6-10

Luke 13:10-13

John 5:1-16

Philippians 2:13

Philippians 4:6

2 Peter 3:18

2 Peter 1:2

1 Corinthians 1:30

Philippians 4:19

1 Peter 2:24

Matthew 11:28-30

# CHAPTER THIRTY-TWO
# JESUS HAS COMPLETED YOUR SUCCESS

Did you know that Jesus wants you to be successful? He died for you to have success and abundance in every area of your life. Grace is God's undeserved, unmerited favor working on your behalf to do what you can't do in your own ability. The Gospel of Grace is the "almost too good to be true" news that you have been made righteous apart from works and that you can completely rest in the finished works of Jesus for every aspect of your life. God takes pleasure in us walking in this favor, but we have to renew our minds to the truth about it. Third John 1:2 says that we can prosper and have health when our souls prosper. A prosperous soul is a soul that is renewed with the Word of God. It is from a renewed mind that a believer can begin to experience this abundant success that has been completed by Jesus.

There are two ways that we can choose to live our lives. We can depend entirely on our own self-effort, performance, and what we perceive as "deserved" favor; or we can depend completely on the undeserved, unmerited favor and blessings of God. We have an abundance of undeserved favor available to us, and it is this grace based prosperity that shows up in the form of success in every area of our lives. We are not supposed to try to perform to get God to prosper us. If you believe Jesus has already prospered you, you don't have to perform for anything. The Gospel of Grace is the ability to get results such as prosperity, healing, salvation, and deliverance. If we believe that our success was already settled two thousand years ago, we can actually begin to walk in it. Under the covenant of grace, our response to what Jesus has done is simply, "I believe! Thank You, Jesus!" It is not about God doing anything else at this point, but about receiving what is finished.

The body of Christ today is involved in too much dead work (the self-effort associated with a law-based mentality). We have everything we could ever need for this life. In fact, God wouldn't have allowed us to be put on this earth if He had not already secured our provision and everything we need for an abundant life. Faith simply takes what has already been done and brings it into present manifestation. Our job is to cooperate with the manifestation when it shows up. Success comes by God's unmerited favor, not what we do in our own ability.

God is a good shepherd. The key to prosperity is knowing you are loved by Him. When you start meditating on how much God loves you, you become unshakeable in your faith; but if you don't believe God loves you, you won't believe in what He has prepared for you and you will blame Him for all the bad that happens in your life. *"And hope maketh not ashamed; because the love of God is shed abroad in our hearts by the Holy Ghost which is given unto us"* (Romans 5:5). This understanding of the love of God in us, for us, and operating through us is the foundation for our success and experiencing the prosperous life that is rightfully ours.

Shifting from a "what God is going to do" mentality to a "what God has already done" mindset is truly the key to success. It is time to stop talking about what is going to happen in the future and start talking about what has already happened through Jesus. We are *already* prosperous, we are already *successful,* and we are *already* rich! It is time to start allowing our faith-response to be in collaboration with what Jesus has already done. We will never be disappointed when we believe the love God has for us. He always delivers on what He promised because He loves us.

### THE IMPORTANCE OF RENEWING THE MIND

Jesus' finished works being manifested in your life is based on your soul being renewed with the Word of God. Renewing the mind is a lifetime process, not a one-time event. It is through renewing our mind that we are able to receive the finished works of Jesus.

A major area of renewal is embracing a grace-based way of thinking versus a law-based way of thinking about why we do what we do for God. For example, in the area of finances, we don't tithe because we are afraid of being cursed if we don't; we tithe out of our love for God. Giving under the covenant of grace is about expressing our appreciation for the truth that Jesus has already taken care of us. God supplies all of our demands, and because of this, we give back to Him (Philippians 4:19). Under grace, financial giving is an act of love, not a requirement. It is a *response* to God's goodness.

Hebrews 9:14 lets us know that the blood of Jesus purges our consciences from dead works. These dead works are the law-based actions we take in an effort to get God to favorably respond to us. Under the law, we deserved hell, but Jesus and His blood paid the sin debt for us. Therefore, we do not have to try to perform well to earn our way to heaven. Jesus took everything we deserved and we now have an abundance of undeserved favor. We are to labor to enter into the rest that belongs to us under this new covenant (Hebrews 4:11). Our minds have been washed with the blood of Jesus so that we can be free from trying to do *anything* outside of believing and receiving from Him.

Christianity is not a religion; it is a relationship. First Corinthians 15:10 says, "*But by the grace of God I am what I am: and his grace which was bestowed upon me was not in vain; but I laboured more abundantly than they all: yet not I, but the grace of God which was with me.*" When you receive the finished works of Jesus, your "doing" will flow effortlessly from a place of grace. You will be doing the works of faith, not the works of the flesh and self-effort, which are manifestations of pride.

When you really understand that you have already been made prosperous by Jesus, you will begin to see the physical manifestation of that inward reality. The Lord was with Joseph, regardless of the fact that he was in prison. Because God was with him, he prospered (Genesis 39:2). Even as a slave, Joseph continued to thrive. Your condition in life doesn't determine your prosperity; your belief in what you already possess through your connection to Jesus does. When the presence of the Lord is with you, you can't help but to prosper and have success. Instead of looking for success in the future, embrace the truth that you are successful *now* because Jesus died for you to have abundant life. Your victory in life comes through resting in the truth of who you are and what belongs to you!

# STUDY QUESTIONS

1. True or False: Jesus actually wants you to be successful.

2. What is God's grace? ______________________________

______________________________

______________________________

______________________________

3. How do we prosper and walk in good health? ______________________________

______________________________

4. True or False: There is a measure of self-effort involved with securing prosperity.

5. What are "dead works"? ______________________________

______________________________

______________________________

6. What is the key to prosperity? ______________________________

______________________________

7. How does success come to us? ____________________

____________________

8. Renewing the mind is a ____________ process, not a one-time event.

9. Under grace, financial giving is ____________________

____________________.

10. Your belief in ____________________

____________________ determines your prosperity.

# ANSWER KEY

1. True
2. His undeserved, unmerited favor working on your behalf to do what you cannot do in your own ability
3. by having a prosperous soul
4. False
5. the law-based actions we take in an effort to get God to respond favorably to us
6. knowing you are loved by God
7. through God's unmerited favor
8. lifetime
9. a response to God's goodness and an act of love
10. what you already possess through your connection to Jesus

**SCRIPTURE REFERENCES**

3 John 1:2

Romans 5:5

Philippians 4:19

Hebrews 9:14

Hebrews 4:11

1 Corinthians 15:10

Genesis 39:2

# CHAPTER THIRTY-THREE
# CEASE FROM WORRY AND ENTER INTO GOD'S REST

If there is one key to entering into the finished works of Jesus, it is to believe in what Jesus has already done for us. To enter into God's rest does not mean inactivity, but it means that while we are doing the things God has called us to do, we maintain our peace and trust in Him. When we have ultimate trust in the finished works of Jesus, we will be empowered with the knowledge that what we need is already taken care of (Hebrews 4:3). We must learn to work *out* of rest. This means that we believe God and what the blood has accomplished for us without question, no matter what things look like in the natural realm.

Trusting God and resting in His love for us is necessary to see the finished works of Jesus materialize in our lives. When we know God loves us, we know that we are already healed, delivered, and blessed, whether we see it or not. When we maintain a position of rest, we become cool, calm, and collected. Being at peace and at rest in Him positions us to prosper in whatever we do (Hebrews 4:2).

We can look to the life of Jesus to see how grace and rest are connected. Luke 2:40 says that as Jesus grew, He became strong spiritually, was filled with wisdom, and the grace of God was upon Him. Now, Romans 5:20 says that when sin abounds, grace abounds even more. Given the Scripture in Romans, the question may come up of how Jesus was able to abound in grace without any sin being in His life (2 Corinthians 5:21). We know that Jesus was sinless, so there is obviously another explanation for why the grace of God was overflowing in His life. If we look at Genesis 6:8, we see the first mention of the grace of God in the Old Testament: "*But Noah found grace in the eyes of the Lord.*" Noah's name actually means "rest." If we plug that meaning into the Scripture, it reads, "But rest found grace in the eyes of the Lord." Here lies the answer to the question of how Jesus abounded in grace: He lived in a perpetual state of rest! The same is true for how we can continually walk in the flow of God's grace; we must rest in Him. Jesus was never stressed about anything He faced. In the garden of Gethsemane, He sweat blood because of the effort He was putting forth to maintain His position of rest (Hebrews 4:11). A place of trust in God is a place of reliance. We are to "hang out" in a place of rest.

Does this concept of rest continue throughout the New Testament? Hebrews 4:9 says, "*There remaineth therefore a rest to the people of God.*" The way we tap into this rest as new-covenant people is by staying consistent in hearing the Word of God. The more we hear the Word, the more faith we will develop in the finished works and the more confidence we will have in what Jesus has done.

There were many people Jesus encountered in His ministry who were in need of healing, deliverance, and provision. For example, there was the man with the withered hand, the woman who had a spirit of infirmity, and the lame man at the pool of Bethesda (Luke 6:6-10; Luke 13:10-13; John 5:1-16). These people gave up trying to change their circumstances after a certain point in time, and it was only then that Jesus offered them a solution to their problems. We can follow their examples. We can release our own efforts to fix our situations, and instead choose to rely on God. We receive when we cease from our labor and allow Jesus to intervene. All three of these people received their miracle on the Sabbath, which is the Jewish day of rest. This signifies that the day we stop striving is the day we will experience a supernatural breakthrough from God.

## SUBMIT AND LET GOD WORK

When it comes to the promises of God, there is absolutely nothing we can do in our own ability that can bring these things to pass. We have to be willing to submit to God and allow His grace to do what we can't do on our own (Philippians 2:13). When it comes to behavior modification, for example, we must rely on the grace of God to do what is impossible through willpower. Bad behavior is actually the result of not knowing your true identity in Christ, but righteousness, holiness, and truth will be expressed through your life and behavior when you are established in your new nature and identity. God is working effectually in your life through Jesus who lives in you. We can't do anything on our own, but God does everything.

This mindset of relying completely on God must translate to every area of our lives. The more we submit ourselves to God, the more we give God the liberty to do what He wants to do in our lives. God wants to know that we need Him! But when we carry stress, worry, and the cares of this life, we block the grace of God from operating. We have been clothed with tremendous power but we must learn to release all of our concerns to God and rest. Praying in the Spirit is a powerful way to do this, and so is simply declaring that you are turning the concern over to God. The objective that you should look to achieve in the midst of every attack is locating the path of rest. Do what you have to do to stay there and watch the manifestations of God's grace for what you need show up (Philippians 4:6, 7).

## GROWING IN THE GRACE OF GOD

Resting in God is directly tied to growing in grace through the knowledge of Jesus Christ. *"But grow in grace, and in the knowledge of our Lord and Saviour Jesus Christ. To him be glory both now and for ever. Amen"* (2 Peter 3:18). The more you know of Jesus, the more you are able to believe in what He has done for you, which leads to more peace and being able to rest. *"Grace and peace be multiplied unto you through the knowledge of God, and of Jesus our Lord"* (2 Peter 1:2). In fact, grace and peace are closely tied together—you can't see grace without having peace. We see more of God's grace and peace when we have more knowledge of Jesus. We must rest in a greater revelation of Jesus as our deliverer, healer, and salvation.

If you don't know who Jesus is and what He has accomplished for you, that lack of knowledge will limit what you can believe Him for. It will also hold back your peace. First Corinthians 1:30 lets us know what we need to know about Jesus: "*But of him are ye in Christ Jesus, who of God is made unto us wisdom, and righteousness, and sanctification, and redemption.*" When you are in Christ, you automatically partake of all that He has, which includes all these things. You are righteous no matter how you miss the mark. Your identity is in Him, which changes everything about you. When you renew your mind to who you are in Christ, your behavior will change.

We are called to live in a perpetual state of rest in the finished works of Jesus because the position of rest that we take today will result in the provision we see tomorrow. Jesus instructs us to take no thought for our daily provisions; but instead seek His kingdom, first, which will cause all those things to be attracted to us (Matthew 6:25, 32, 33). When we are anxious, stressed out, and carrying care, we are basically communicating that we don't trust Jesus; but when we rest and trust God, we let Him know that we are relying on Him. Under God's care there is no lack. We must remind ourselves that we are not the source of our prosperity; we are not trying to help ourselves, expecting God to assist when we engage in self-effort.

God has made His peace available to all people. Religion tells us to be self-reliant, but a thriving relationship with Jesus Christ is all about relying only on Him as the source. In Matthew 11:28, 29, Jesus says, "*Come unto me, all ye that labour and are heavy laden, and I will give you rest. Take my yoke upon you, and learn of me; for I am meek and lowly in heart: and ye shall find rest unto your souls.*" God doesn't put burdens on you. His yoke is easy. He doesn't want you to sweat; He wants you to rest. Your labor isn't going to get you to the places God wants you to be. Be still and know that God is God, and that everything you need has been provided for (Psalm 46:10). There is no need to worry when you rest in the finished works of Jesus Christ.

# STUDY QUESTIONS

1. True or False: Resting means doing nothing.

2. What happens when we trust in the finished works of Jesus? ____________________
____________________________________________________________
____________________________________________________________
____________________________________________________________

3. ______________________________ and ______________________________
are mandatory for us to see the manifestation of the finished works of Jesus.

4. When we maintain a position of rest, we become ______________________________
______________________________________________.

5. How did grace abound in Jesus' life? ______________________________
____________________________________________________________
____________________________________________________________

6. A place of trust is a place of ______________________________________.

7. How do we tap into the rest of God as new covenant people? ________________

_______________________________________________

_______________________________________________

8. What was the common thread between the three sick people who received from Jesus? _______________________________________________

_______________________________________________

9. What is the objective we should look to achieve in the midst of every attack?

_______________________________________________

10. True or False: God has made His peace available to all people.

# ANSWER KEY

1. False
2. We will be empowered with the knowledge that what we need is already taken care of.
3. Trusting God; resting in His love for us
4. cool, calm, and collected
5. He stayed in a continual place of rest.
6. reliance
7. by staying consistent in hearing the Word of God
8. They gave up trying to get results in their own ability.
9. rest
10. True

**SCRIPTURE REFERENCES**

Hebrews 4:2, 3

Luke 2:40

Romans 5:20

2 Corinthians 5:21

Genesis 6:8

Hebrews 4:11

Hebrews 4:9

Luke 6:6-10

Luke 13:10-13

John 5:1-16

Philippians 2:13

Philippians 4:6-7

2 Peter 3:18

2 Peter 1:2

1 Corinthians 1:30

Matthew 6:25, 32, 33

Matthew 11:28, 29

Psalm 46:10

# CHAPTER THIRTY-FOUR
# HOW TO DEVELOP CONFIDENCE IN THE FINISHED WORKS OF JESUS

If relying solely on the finished works of Jesus is essential to seeing the manifestation of those works in our lives, then it is critical for us to develop confidence in what He has already done for us. But what happens when a believer doesn't have confidence? How can one develop the confidence necessary to walk in the finished works on a daily basis? The first thing to understand is that the only way to walk in the rest that comes with relying on the finished works of Jesus is to *believe.* Those who believe, trust, and rely on what Jesus has accomplished are the ones who enter into that rest. The place of rest is the place of manifestation.

Every believer must be in a place of rest in order to find the grace needed during a time of trouble. Most of the things that haven't manifested in our lives have been stopped because we have gotten into stress, worry, and carrying the cares of life rather than resting. However, a life that pursues rest is a life that will experience the manifestation of the finished works of Jesus. Remember that rest is not inactivity; it is relying on Him while you do what you do every day. It is getting up to go to work while maintaining an attitude of peace and trust in God to provide for all your needs. It is factoring Jesus into everything and knowing that His peace and joy have been given to you so that you can stay at rest when tempted to become consumed with the care of a situation.

When you enter into rest, you are there because you have trust and confidence in what He has done. Just like you can't rest in a chair that you know can't support you, you can't rest in God if you have no confidence in Him. Isaiah 30:15 says, "*For thus saith the Lord God, the Holy One of Israel; In returning and rest shall ye be saved; in quietness and in confidence shall be your strength: and ye would not.*" If you want to be delivered, rescued, and prospered, it is going to be in the place of rest; and if you want the strength to accomplish this, you must be confident. There is a quietness associated with confidence in God. It is an indication that you truly are trusting in Him. The enemy knows you have an advantage over him, which is why he wants to get you focused on situations and circumstances that attack your confidence. Don't allow him to do it. Be confident in the finished works of Jesus Christ. This is where your strength lies.

Hebrews 10:35, 36 shows us the value of confidence. It says, "*Cast not away therefore your confidence, which hath great recompence of reward. For ye have need of patience, that, after ye have done the will of God, ye might receive the promise.*" There is a compensation that comes from having confidence in the finished works of Jesus. It is the promise of God coming to pass in your life. Satan attacks confidence because, when he does, your rest is disrupted. Disrupted rest leads to no manifestation happening in your life. When you have no manifestation, other people cannot see the glory of God being displayed, which affects their trust in Him, as well. This is why it is so important for us to live a life in which others can see us resting and trusting in God.

In order not to cast away your confidence, you need patience. Now, patience doesn't mean you are putting up with something. It means remaining consistently, constantly the same, unchanging in the face of circumstances and situations that are contrary to the Word. When patience is allowed to have her perfect work, you keep your confidence out on the field. Refusing to quit on your faith is what puts you over into seeing results.

Many Christians have an endurance problem when it comes to allowing their faith to carry them through to breakthrough. When Peter walked on the water, he was operating in strong faith; but the moment he began to pay attention to the waves and the wind that raged around him, he began to sink (Matthew 14:22-33). Peter's faith was weak at that point because he did not allow his strong faith to continue. We can learn a valuable lesson about confidence from this. Our faith has to be backed by patience in order to continue working long enough to see the end of our faith. Never bring your faith in from the field before being totally satisfied with the results that you are believing God for.

Hebrews 10:38, 39 says, "*Now the just shall live by faith: but if any man draw back, my soul shall have no pleasure in him. But we are not of them who draw back unto perdition; but of them that believe to the saving of the soul.*" The just are those who have been declared righteous by God. They live by faith, or confidence, in God and His Word. We live confidently in the finished works of Jesus Christ and we don't draw back.

Confidence means getting up every day expecting to see a promise of God come to pass in your life. It is a refusal to settle for anything less. Believers are not to get disappointed and quit because our God never lets us down. When we put our patience to work, it empowers our faith to go the distance.

The book of Acts gives the ultimate picture of what it looks like not to throw away your confidence in the midst of challenging circumstances:

> But not long after there arose against it a tempestuous wind, called Euroclydon... And we being exceedingly tossed with a tempest, the next day they lightened the ship...And when neither sun nor stars in many days appeared, and no small tempest lay on us, all hope that we should be saved was then taken away. But after long abstinence Paul stood forth in the midst of them, and said, Sirs, ye should have hearkened unto me, and not have loosed from Crete, and to have gained this harm and loss. And now I exhort you to be of good cheer: for there shall be no loss of any man's life among you, but of the ship. For there stood by me this night the angel of God, whose I am, and whom I serve, Saying, Fear not, Paul; thou must be brought before Caesar: and, lo, God hath given thee all them that sail with thee. Wherefore, sirs, be of good cheer: for I believe God, that it shall be even as it was told me (Acts 27:14, 18, 20-25).

God was letting Paul know that nothing was going to happen to him because he had a destiny. Paul was able to be of good cheer in the midst of a hurricane because he believed God through it all. When you believe God, you are able to walk through life in good cheer. You trust in what Jesus said to you and believe that things will turn out just as He promised.

*"Above all, taking the shield of faith, wherewith ye shall be able to quench all the fiery darts of the wicked"* (Ephesians 6:16). The key is making sure that we lift up our shield when the darts come. We do this by declaring the Word of God when Satan tries to inject thoughts of doubt and fear. This is a way to keep our patience working as we wait for the manifestation of the promise. Shutting down the attacks of the enemy with the Word of God will enable our faith to have the endurance it needs. If we are willing to stand forever, we won't have to stand very long.

*"If any of you lack wisdom, let him ask of God, that giveth to all men liberally, and upbraideth not; and it shall be given him. But let him ask in faith, nothing wavering. For he that wavereth is like a wave of the sea driven with the wind and tossed. For let not that man think that he shall receive any thing of the Lord. A double minded man is unstable in all his ways"* (James 1:5-8). We are to ask God for wisdom, in faith, and refuse to waver once the request is submitted to God. The person who wavers is double-minded and should not expect to receive anything from God. The enemy banks on the double-minded Christian remaining in a place of doubt and unbelief because it will cause that person to lose focus on God. When this happens, manifestation is canceled.

Confidence in God and His Word is absolutely vital to walking in the finished works of Christ. This is the key. God will do *anything* for the person who believes, so it is up to us to feed our faith with His Word on a continual basis and refuse to be moved from what He has said. The more we renew our minds with the Word and meditate on it, the more our confidence will soar. We will find ourselves living from a place of unshakable confidence. When the storms of life show up, they won't be able to move us. God's Word is the foundation upon which our confidence is built. Patience allows our faith to outlast the circumstances and situations that seek to disrupt our focus and prevent us from resting in what God promised. *"But let patience have her perfect work, that ye may be perfect and entire, wanting nothing"* (James 1:4). Let patience have its perfect work so that your faith materializes as the abundant life that belongs to you as a beneficiary of grace.

# STUDY QUESTIONS

1. What is required to walk in the rest of God? ____________________

   ____________________

2. How do we find the grace we need in times of trouble? ____________________

   ____________________

3. Why are a lot of blessings prevented from manifesting in our lives? ____________________

   ____________________

   ____________________

4. Jesus has given us His ____________________ and ____________________ so that, when we are tempted, we can remain at rest.

5. According to Isaiah 30:15, what is an indicator of confidence? ____________________

6. Why are we instructed not to cast away our confidence? ____________________

   ____________________

   ____________________

   ____________________

7. Why does Satan attack our confidence? ______________________________

_______________________________________________

_______________________________________________

_______________________________________________

8. Why do many Christians fail to see the end of their faith? ______________

_______________________________________________

9. Our faith needs to be backed by ______________________________.

10. How do we quench the fiery darts of Satan? ______________________

_______________________________________________

# ANSWER KEY

1. belief
2. by being in a place of rest
3. because of stress, worry, and carrying cares
4. peace; joy
5. quietness
6. because we will be compensated for it in the form of the promises of God manifesting in our lives
7. because it disrupts us from our place of rest, which hinders manifestation
8. because their faith has no endurance or ability to last
9. patience
10. by declaring the Word of God

**SCRIPTURE REFERENCES**

Isaiah 30:15

Hebrews 10:35, 36, 38, 39

Matthew 14:22-33

Acts 27:14, 18, 20-25

Ephesians 6:16

James 1:4-8

# CHAPTER THIRTY-FIVE
# HOW TO OVERCOME SHAME

If there is one thing that is stopping believers from walking in the fullness of what God has called them to do, it is shame. Shame is an emotion that has the potential to derail us if we allow it to. In fact, Satan would like nothing more than to keep us paralyzed in condemnation and shame, rather than move forward into the destiny that God has prepared for each of us. The key to overcoming shame is understanding what it is and how Jesus has defeated it. When you do, you will be able to fulfill the will of God for your life without fail.

Shame is a hindrance to success and to the plan of God for your life. It is an emotion caused by a consciousness of guilt or shortcoming. Shame will move you to hide yourself in an attempt to hide your shame. The good news is that God has already set you free from it through Jesus' redemptive work on the cross. Jesus took on shame so that we wouldn't have to take it on. To go further, Jesus became the object of *our* shame so that we wouldn't have to be subjected to eternal shame for our sins. Jesus submitted to shame so that we wouldn't have to.

Isaiah 50:6, 7 is a powerful Scripture that gives insight into this issue of shame and how Jesus would become shame on our behalf: *"I gave my back to the smiters, and my cheeks to them that plucked off the hair: I hid not my face from shame and spitting. For the Lord God will help me; therefore shall I not be confounded: therefore have I set my face like a flint, and I know that I shall not be ashamed."*

We often lose sight of the brutality that Jesus endured on our behalf, but the Scriptures always bring us back to the truth of what Jesus went through. In this passage, we see the truth. Jesus willingly allowed Himself to be shamed in every possible way so that we wouldn't have to walk around in shame for the times we miss the mark. The Word of God says that He gave His face to His enemies to be beaten, spit on, and even have his facial hair pulled out. He allowed Himself to be beaten mercilessly, and in the midst of it all, He trusted God to be His defense. He was confident that through all of the shaming that He endured, He would come out victorious and wouldn't be ashamed in the end. Jesus did this for all of us; He became our shame because He loved us so much.

Jesus also suffered the shame of rejection. *"And about the ninth hour Jesus cried with a loud voice, saying, Eli, Eli, lama sabachthani? that is to say, My God, my God, why hast thou forsaken me?"* (Matthew 27:46). You see, when Jesus went to the cross, He didn't just take on sin; He *became* it. Because He became sin, the Father turned His back on Jesus in those moments. Jesus was accepting the full punishment and rejection of God while becoming the ultimate sin-sacrifice. He went through the shame of rejection so that we would never be rejected by the Father when we receive Jesus into our hearts. Jesus is literally glued to you when you accept Him as your Lord and Savior. God forsook Jesus so that He would never forsake us.

First Peter 3:18 says, *"For Christ also hath once suffered for sins, the just for the unjust, that he might bring us to God, being put to death in the flesh, but quickened by the Spirit."* Every sin that you could ever commit, Jesus suffered for it (Isaiah 53:4). When we really get a revelation of this, it becomes clear that we can't allow shame to consume us when we sin. We haven't just been relieved from the shame of sin; we have been released from it.

## DO YOU BELIEVE?

It is possible to be a Christian and be undeveloped in your belief in what Jesus has done for you. This is why so many believers live in condemnation and can never really rise up into the fullness of their righteousness in everyday life. Shame is something that you take in, but Jesus has already accepted it on your behalf. What do you believe?

Often we think that humility is being quiet and not saying too much, but humility is actually submitting to the Word of God and God's way of doing things. True humility is submitting to the truth of what Jesus has done for us. The Word lets us know that Jesus has handled our shame. Second Corinthians 5:21 says, "*For he hath made him to be sin for us, who knew no sin; that we might be made the righteousness of God in him,*" and Romans 9:33 says, "*As it is written, Behold, I lay in Sion a stumblingstone and rock of offence: and whosoever believeth on him shall not be ashamed.*" Meditating on these truths will allow you to become grounded in the freedom that Jesus has granted you.

You can't build anything on a weak foundation. If your foundation of righteousness as a believer is not strong, you will not be able to stand in the face of the condemnation the enemy will try to heap on you. When you carry shame, it demonstrates pride and hinders God's ability to help you. The horrors of your life come when you try to take on something that Jesus has taken away. *"Comfort ye, comfort ye my people, saith your God. Speak ye comfortably to Jerusalem, and cry unto her, that her warfare is accomplished, that her iniquity is pardoned: for she hath received of the Lord's hand double for all her sins"* (Isaiah 40:1, 2). The truth is that if you are in Him, you have been made the righteousness of God. When you believe on Jesus, you will not be ashamed. When you live from this place of realizing the magnitude of Jesus' sacrifice, you won't be confounded or ashamed. Only believe!

To go a little deeper, shame is the sense that you've failed in the eyes of someone else. It is the intense pain and feeling of unworthiness and being disconnected. It is the feeling of being unlovable. When you feel unworthy, you feel paralyzed and the devil will capitalize on this to the fullest extent. You will push people away because, on a core level, you don't believe you're worthy of love. You will shame others because you feel terrible about yourself. Shame essentially convinces you that you're worthless.

While guilt is a preoccupation with feeling bad about what you've done, shame is seeing yourself as a failure because of who you are. It is one of the most toxic emotions a person can hold on to.

In order to overcome shame, it is critical that you begin to meditate on the truth that, as long as you are in Christ, you can never be a failure. Jesus has taken all the shame away and has made a way for every believer to live a shame-free life. *"Blotting out the handwriting of ordinances that was against us, which was contrary to us, and took it out of the way, nailing it to his cross"* (Colossians 2:14). By believing that you receive this liberation from shame, you open yourself up to a life of peace, healing, and restoration, even from past mistakes. You have no business carrying shame when you have received the free gift of salvation. *"For your shame ye shall have double; and for confusion they shall rejoice in their portion: therefore in their land they shall possess the double: everlasting joy shall be unto them"* (Isaiah 61:7). Receive freedom from shame today and know that you are accepted by the Father through your relationship with Jesus Christ.

# STUDY QUESTIONS

1. True or False: Jesus has already delivered every believer from shame, no matter what sin they have committed.

2. What is shame? ______________________________________________
______________________________________________________________

3. What will shame move you to do? ______________________________

4. Jesus became the ____________________ of our ____________________.

5. True or False: Carrying cares and shame makes you humble.

6. True or False: Guilt and shame are the same thing.

7. What is guilt? ______________________________________________
______________________________________________________________

8. You cannot stand in the face of the condemnation the enemy will try to heap on you if you are not established on a foundation of ____________________.

9. How do you overcome shame? ____________________

____________________

10. People who carry shame:

    A. push people away.

    B. shame others.

    C. feel worthless.

    D. all of the above.

# ANSWER KEY

1. True
2. seeing yourself as a failure because of something you've done
3. hide yourself
4. object; shame
5. False
6. False
7. feeling bad about something you've done
8. righteousness
9. by meditating on the truth that Jesus has taken your shame away
10. D

### SCRIPTURE REFERENCES

Isaiah 50:6, 7

Matthew 27:46

1 Peter 3:18

Isaiah 53:4

2 Corinthians 5:21

Romans 9:33

Isaiah 40:1-2

Colossians 2:14

Isaiah 61:7

# CHAPTER THIRTY-SIX
# THE CONSEQUENCES FOR NOT DEALING WITH SHAME

Shame is a killer. It kills dreams, vision, purpose, and progression. If it is left unchecked, it will annihilate everything that God desires to do in and through our lives. Satan uses it as a tool in his arsenal of destruction. Believers must reject shame and receive the freedom that Jesus has secured for us, by faith. *"I gave my back to the smiters, and my cheeks to them that plucked off the hair: I hid not my face from shame and spitting. For the Lord God will help me; therefore shall I not be confounded: therefore have I set my face like a flint, and I know that I shall not be ashamed"* (Isaiah 50:6, 7). Everyone has done things they aren't proud of and there is always something from our past that we may feel ashamed about; however, by meditating on and becoming grounded in what Jesus has done for you, shame cannot stick around. By studying the Scriptures and really allowing them to renew your mind, you can overcome shame and not become subject to its consequences.

The consequences of shame come when we refuse to humble ourselves and cast our cares on the Lord. When we take on shame and carry it in our daily lives, the repercussions are devastating and will infect every relationship and situation. Shame is a sense of failure in the eyes of God and other people. It isn't just a feeling that you failed, but that you failed and others saw it. It is the intense feeling of being unworthy, disconnected, and unlovable by God and people. There is a difference between feeling the guilt of something you did and feeling ashamed of who you are. Shame hits the very core of your personhood and severely impairs your ability to do anything significant for God because you are too ashamed of yourself. It is truly a poisonous way to live.

There are several things that are present in the life of a person who is carrying shame. These things are by-products of not receiving the redemptive work of Christ and allowing the truth of that work to renew your mind. First, shame will cause paranoia. When you are in shame, you will be paranoid about people and how they view you. There have been instances of people leaving their church because they were ashamed of something they did and felt like everyone knew about it. The truth is that, most likely, "everyone" did not know about it; but even if they knew, they definitely didn't care enough about it to allow that thing to affect their own personal life. But shame will do that to you. It will start speaking to you and telling you that others are viewing you a certain way that they most likely are not. It will make you paranoid about others so that you do not enter into the vital relationships that God intended you to have. When we are ashamed, we tend to think that others are judging us or talking about us. It causes us to shy away from fellowship. Clearly this is a tactic of the enemy to keep people from connecting in ways that can be a blessing to them.

The second thing shame does is tie you to your past. A person who is carrying shame is tied to whatever happened in their past that brought the shame in the first place. As a result, they are unable to move forward into the glorious future God has for them. The ties to the past are strengthened by the shame they feel and it is difficult for them to experience the fresh life of freedom and blessings. God wants us to know that He can take the bad pieces of our past and bring them together with the good pieces to make a beautiful masterpiece. This enables us to use all of the good and the bad we experience to relate to people and minister to them. We should not look at our past bad decisions or lifestyles as things to be ashamed of, but parts of our story that God will use to help someone else.

Third, shame extinguishes hope. If you want to know what a hopeless person looks like, look at someone who is carrying shame in their heart and mind. You simply cannot have any hope that God will use you or bless you if you are walking around in shame over something that you have done or something that has happened to you. Jesus carried all the shame of offense and rejection so that you wouldn't have to (Romans 9:33). Do you believe what Jesus said in His Word about taking your shame, or will you continue to stay connected to someone else's words or the devil's words that are whispered to your mind? Faith comes by hearing, and hearing the Word of God (Romans 10:17). When you make it a priority to hear only what God has said about you, it will build your confidence and give you hope that He has a wonderful life of abundance prepared for you. Nothing can separate you from that life except your refusal to let go of the shame.

Finally, shame becomes a weight and a burden. There are so many people who are walking around burdened down by their past, their sins, and the experiences in their lives that have caused them to cower in shame. So many believers are paralyzed because they carry these weights. God didn't design us to carry anything except His glory! The weight and burden of shame is too much to bear, and why would you want to? Jesus bore that burden on the cross so you wouldn't have to. Letting go of shame is the most powerful thing you can do for your spirit and soul.

### THE FIRST WEAPON SATAN USED

Did you know that shame was the first weapon Satan used in the garden of Eden against mankind? Genesis 3:10 documents Adam's first reaction to his sin: "*And he said, I heard thy voice in the garden, and I was afraid, because I was naked; and I hid myself.*" Adam and Eve hid from God when they missed it, instead of simply repenting to God. They were so ashamed that they hid from their loving creator, which created more separation. They were hiding from God and hiding from the shame of their actions. Adam and Eve give us a picture of what not to do when we miss the mark. Instead of hiding from God (which is impossible anyway), move beyond the sin or mistake, and receive forgiveness from God. I wonder what would have happened to Adam and Eve if they had chosen to move past the shame and simply run to God. What is on the other side of your shame that you haven't discovered? God wants to restore everything shame has tried to steal from you, but you have to be willing to release it in order to receive that restoration from Him.

**FIRST THINGS FIRST**

In order to get to the root of shame, we have to deal with pride. Someone may say, how is pride at the root of shame? The answer is simple. Pride is a refusal to heed God's Word and His way of doing things. If He told us in His Word that Jesus has taken our shame and we continue to carry shame, refusing to release it, we are pursuing our own way of handling this emotion instead of choosing God's way. This is pride, and *"When pride cometh, then cometh shame"* (Proverbs 11:2). So, if you're dealing with shame, trace it back to some area of your life that you refused God's way. *"Humble yourselves therefore under the mighty hand of God, that he may exalt you in due time"* (1 Peter 5:6). Humility refers to the person who will submit to God's way of doing things. If you are struggling with shame, ask God to help you not to walk in pride and show you areas of pride that you may be harboring. You cannot be humble when you are carrying worry, stress, and shame; and when you are in pride, you block yourself from being able to receive God's grace in a time of trouble.

When you battle shame, it is really an issue of unbelief. That is something that you must resolve by getting plugged into the truth about what Jesus did for you on the cross. He paid the ultimate price for your shame and His grace is more than enough for anything you are going through. When you are weak, the Bible says that you are the strongest because His power is working in and through you to help you overcome (2 Corinthians 12:9). Don't allow Satan to steal your confidence in your righteousness by carrying shame. Rejoice in what Jesus has accomplished so that you can move forward in a shame-free life, no matter what has happened in your past.

# STUDY QUESTIONS

1. Shame is a weapon Satan uses to ______________________________.

2. What does shame do? ______________________________

   ______________________________

   ______________________________

3. True or False: The core issue of shame is unbelief.

4. True or False: Shame was the first weapon Satan used in the garden of Eden against Adam and Eve.

5. How could Adam and Eve have handled the fact that they sinned when God approached them? ______________________________

   ______________________________

6. ______________________________ is the root of shame.

7. What is pride? ______________________________

   ______________________________

   ______________________________

8. What is humility? ______________________________________________

______________________________________________

9. True or False: Pride will keep you from seeing grace in a time of trouble.

# ANSWER KEY

1. destroy
2. It causes paranoia, ties you to your past, extinguishes hope, and becomes a weight and a burden.
3. True
4. True
5. repented instead of hiding
6. Pride
7. a refusal to submit to God's Word and His way of doing things
8. submitting to God's Word
9. True

**SCRIPTURE REFERENCES**

Isaiah 50:6-7

Romans 9:33

Romans 10:17

Genesis 3:10

Proverbs 11:2

1 Peter 5:6

2 Corinthians 12:9

# CHAPTER THIRTY-SEVEN
# WAYS WE BATTLE SHAME

One of the weapons in Satan's arsenal that can sabotage a person's future is the weapon of shame. This is because shame absolutely moves you away from the call of God on your life. When you are ashamed, you feel worthless, unlovable, and incapable of fulfilling anything God calls you to do. You are paralyzed by the sense of being a failure as a person. Fortunately, God has made a way out of the shame trap. *"Fear not; for thou shalt not be ashamed: neither be thou confounded; for thou shalt not be put to shame: for thou shalt forget the shame of thy youth, and shalt not remember the reproach of thy widowhood any more"* (Isaiah 54:4). If you have received Jesus as your Lord and Savior, you have been delivered from shame and all of its consequences. Because of what Jesus did on the cross (becoming an object of shame for our sin), we no longer have to carry shame. In fact, to carry it after Jesus has taken the burden of shame away is to walk in pride (Proverbs 11:2). There is forgiveness for any and every sin you have committed (Psalm 130:4). God promises in His Word to have mercy on you (Isaiah 55:6, 7). Mercy is when you don't experience the judgment you deserve. In order to walk free from shame, we must focus on the voice of mercy and not the voice of the enemy trying to shame us. God sees your value and wants you to move forward in what He has called you to do.

Getting free from shame requires belief in what Jesus has already done. Acts 10:43 holds a promise to all those who put their faith in Christ: "*To him give all the prophets witness, that through his name whosoever believeth in him shall receive remission of sins.*" Simply put, when you believe in the name of Jesus and what He has done for you, your sins aren't just atoned for or covered; they are completely obliterated. In other words, God doesn't even see any of your sins anymore because they have been wiped out. Since you no longer carry sin in your spirit, you have no reason to carry shame.

You may be thinking, "Well, I sinned last night, and I'm ashamed about it." Stop right there. You may have missed the mark but, if you are a believer, God doesn't see you as a sinner. When you sin, simply receive His forgiveness by faith and continue to stand in your righteousness in Christ. The more time you spend meditating on your new nature of righteousness and holiness, the less attractive that sin will become; and if you do sin, you can get right back up and keep moving forward with Jesus without condemnation. *"For I will be merciful to their unrighteousness, and their sins and their iniquities will I remember no more"* (Hebrews 8:12). The Bible promises that God is merciful toward us and there is no sin that God isn't powerful enough to deal with in your life. There is no need to live a life that is marked by shame.

### Three Areas of Shame

While there are many instances of shame and different ways people deal with it, there are generally three areas in which the believer battles shame:

1. Shame for past sin
2. Shame for glorifying God
3. Shame for something that you didn't do

Let's take a look at all three.

The first area is probably one of the most common. Shame for past sin is rampant in the body of Christ; however, it is a function of pride to carry something that Jesus has already taken away from you. *"But Israel shall be saved in the Lord with an everlasting salvation: ye shall not be ashamed nor confounded world without end"* (Isaiah 45:17). When Jesus went to the cross, He didn't just take on your shame, He *became* shame and sin. He was made the object of complete ridicule as an act of His will, in order to ensure that we didn't have to ever carry shame for past sins. Many believers are carrying shame from things they did before they even got born again! They are locked into feelings of unworthiness and condemnation because they are so ashamed of their past lifestyles or decisions. There is good news today! The good news is that God's grace has been made available through faith. When you receive Christ, you are made a completely new spiritual creature. You are cleansed of all your sin and God doesn't even remember what you did. If you sin as a Christian, you can receive the cleansing of Jesus' blood on a continual basis. You can be free from any feelings of condemnation when you miss the mark because your sin has been wiped out. Many times we keep ourselves locked in a jail cell of shame when God has set us free.

The second area of shame that many Christians battle is shame for glorifying God. This is something that believers *must* deal with. We should never be ashamed of the things that glorify God, or be ashamed to praise Him or talk about Him openly. Second Timothy 1:12 says, *"For the which cause I also suffer these things: nevertheless I am not ashamed: for I know whom I have believed, and am persuaded that he is able to keep that which I have committed unto him against that day."* The apostle Paul is our example of the kind of attitude we need to take toward the things of God. He boldly declares that he is not ashamed of anything he has gone through that glorifies God, because he *knows who he believes.* You see, getting rid of shame is all about who and what you believe. When you know Jesus and what He has done for you, you simply cannot be ashamed to glorify Him, even if the things you go through are difficult.

God has been too good to us to be ashamed of Him in any form or fashion. There is something that happens when you are able to praise God with reckless abandon, unconcerned with how others will look at you or see you. In fact, there is restoration on the other side of your unashamed praise. Don't be afraid to talk about God, proclaim Him to people, and let the world know that you serve Jesus! There is no shame in sharing the Gospel because it is the power to bring salvation and life to others (Romans 1:16).

The third area in which people battle shame is for something they didn't do. This usually comes from people who are full of shame themselves and they try to load you with shame. There are times when you did not do anything to dishonor God, but others will try to shame you because they feel terrible themselves. For example, God may be prospering you because you have honored Him with your finances, but someone may try to make you feel bad about acquiring wealth because of their own issues surrounding shame and financial blessings. Whether it is finances or any other area, never receive anyone else's shame being heaped on you. Reject any form of shame, whether it comes from yourself or someone else, by believing God and what He promised as it relates to taking away your shame. Have confidence that all efforts others make to put shame on you will undoubtedly fail.

### BELIEVING ON JESUS

Shame is overcome through belief, not just believing *in* Jesus but by living a life spent believing *on* Him (Romans 10:11). To walk in shame is essentially to say, "I know what He said He did, but I don't believe it." We can't call ourselves believers and then refuse to believe what Jesus has done for us. *"[W]hosoever believeth on him shall not be ashamed"* (Romans 9:33). You will always find out what you really believe when an issue happens in your life that others know about. These types of situations put your faith to the test, but they also reveal your belief system. God wants us to become so established in who we are in Christ that no situation, circumstance, sin, or challenge can cause us to walk in shame. It takes renewing your mind and a commitment to believe on Jesus and His finished works. When you commit to eradicating a shame-filled consciousness, you will find yourself able to move forward in all the wonderful things God has for you. Nobody remembers how you start, but what they do remember is how you finish. We want to go to heaven victorious, knowing that we overcame shame in all of its forms. Refuse to be paralyzed by shame. Instead make a quality decision to live boldly for God no matter what your past or present looks like. God has set you free, now walk in it!

# STUDY QUESTIONS

1. Shame is a ________________________________ Satan uses to ________________________________ your future.

2. When you are ashamed, you feel _______________________________________________________________________________________________________________________.

3. Getting free from shame requires _______________________________________________________________________________________________________________________.

4. True or False: No sin is beyond God's forgiveness.

5. What is mercy? ___________________________________________________________________

6. Overcoming shame requires that you move ________________________________.

7. Who receives remission of sins? ___________________________________________________________________

8. What are the three areas in which believers battle shame? ______________________

______________________________________________

______________________________________________

______________________________________________

9. Why do people try to load others with shame? ______________________

______________________________________________

10. Shame is an issue of ______________________________________.

# ANSWER KEY

1. weapon; sabotage
2. worthless, unlovable, and incapable of fulfilling what God has called you to do
3. belief in what Jesus has already done
4. True
5. when you don't experience the judgment you deserve
6. forward
7. all those who believe in the name of Jesus
8. shame for past sin, shame for glorifying God, and shame that others put on them
9. because they are full of shame themselves
10. unbelief

**SCRIPTURE REFERENCES**

Isaiah 54:4
Proverbs 11:2
Psalm 130:4
Isaiah 55:6-7
Acts 10:43
Hebrews 8:12
2 Timothy 1:12
Romans 1:16
Isaiah 45:17
Romans 10:11
Romans 9:33

# CHAPTER THIRTY-EIGHT
# SET FREE FROM SHAME

Walking around in shame as a believer is a nightmare that causes you to shy away from what God has designed for your life (Ezra 9:5, 6). The promises, destiny, and blessings God has provided for you become blocked when shame is ruling your life. The truth is that God wants you to have a working revelation that you have been set free from shame! Jesus became a shame substitute for us when He offered Himself up as a sacrifice for our sins (Isaiah 50:6, 7). When you realize that Jesus put on shame so that you don't have to put it on, you are able to release the shame and condemnation that you are carrying and experience the liberty of living a shame-free life. This is the life that God intends for you.

Shame is a sense of failure at who you are as a person, and it involves feeling disconnected and unlovable by people and God. While guilt is feeling bad about something you've done, shame is feeling bad about who you are. It can lead you to be paranoid and cause you to see yourself as bad so that you believe everyone else is bad as well. Shame ties you to your past and paralyzes you from moving into your future. It is the number one weapon that Satan uses against Christians, but when you live a lifestyle of believing on Jesus and His finished works, you will reject the voice of shame.

There are several sources of shame that we must be aware of. It can come through accidents that take place, victimization such as abuse, humiliation, or rejection, or inherited shame that comes from things like your background, how you feel about your looks, your family, etc. Satan uses all of these things to try to violate our worth, make us feel less than others, and make us feel unworthy in the sight of God. He causes us to feel like we can't live up to the expectations that people have of us.

In order to combat these kinds of shame and be set free from them, we have to take some proactive steps. The first step is to find out what the Word of God has to say. Renewing the mind occurs when we find the Scriptures that relate to our specific situations. We begin to meditate on them on a consistent basis until they change our thinking and, ultimately, our behavior. A lot of the shame that people deal with comes from the outside in, from them feeling shamed about something they have no control over. Reminding yourself of how God sees you is a key to overcoming shame.

Psalm 139:14 is a beautiful Scripture that communicates our worth in the eyes of God: "*I will praise thee; for I am fearfully and wonderfully made: marvellous are thy works; and that my soul knoweth right well.*" The message here is clear: you are God's masterpiece! What an encouraging Scripture to combat shame in any form. No matter what your background, appearance, or family history, God has uniquely formed you for a purpose. You are the apple of His eye.

Shame can paralyze you when you refuse to let go of things from your past and when you feel you haven't met the expectations of others. Getting free from people's opinions and plugging into *God's* opinion of you is going to be a key to keeping the past in the past and preventing it from following you into your future. Your past sins do not have any bearing on the amazing future God has planned for you. Micah 7:19 says, "*He will turn again, he will have compassion upon us; he will subdue our iniquities; and thou wilt cast all their sins into the depths of the sea.*" What a promise! God says that He will have compassion on us and cast our sins into the depths of the sea. If shame from your past is tormenting you, this promise from God wipes it out. You simply have to believe and receive it.

The apostle Paul had many things from his past that the devil tried to torment him with after he received Christ. Before he became the apostle Paul, he was Saul of Tarsus, a religious Pharisee who took pleasure in persecuting Christians and having them imprisoned and killed. When he had his encounter with Jesus, all of that changed; he became a new man and began to preach the Gospel unashamedly. However, you can imagine the mental battles that Paul must have endured when the enemy brought up his past. Nevertheless, in Philippians 3:13, he said, *"Brethren, I count not myself to have apprehended: but this one thing I do, forgetting those things which are behind, and reaching forth unto those things which are before."* This is the attitude of a believer who rejects shame and the mistakes of his or her past. It is the attitude of a victorious Christian who believes in the finished works of Christ.

## THREE WAYS TO OVERCOME SHAME

Now that we understand what shame is and the ways it tries to derail us, let's look at three key ways to overcome it once and for all. We know that believing in what Jesus has done for us is the foundation for overcoming shame. *"Looking unto Jesus the author and finisher of our faith; who for the joy that was set before him endured the cross, despising the shame, and is set down at the right hand of the throne of God"* (Hebrews 12:2). There are some practical ways to put this into action. First, you must despise shame and refuse to let it influence your identity. It is the attitude of saying, "I may have failed, but I'm not a failure." Shame is a despicable fool, unworthy of our attention. Romans 10:11 says, "*For the scripture saith, Whosoever believeth on him shall not be ashamed.*"

Second, you have to *banish* shame. In other words, don't let it influence your actions toward others. Hurt people hurt other people, and shame begets more shame. When you are ashamed, and you don't deal with it, you will put your shame on other people, which is not fair. People who feel low will try to lower others. Shame will minister to you to tear people down so that you can feel better and higher than them. This is not how God wants us to live. His eternal love and honor will overcome all shame and allow us to express that love to others. Getting out of shame is essential to building and maintaining relationships with people.

Finally, you must reject shame in any form that it comes to you. Whether it is through the devil speaking thoughts to your mind, other people trying to shame you, or you shaming yourself for whatever reason, do not tolerate shame. At the same time, don't let shame influence your perception of others by stigmatizing them. God loves you and He loves other people. It is not His will that anyone live a shame-driven life.

The Gospel, which is the message of God's grace through the finished works of Jesus, is the power of God unto salvation (Romans 1:16). It is the reason why we have access to freedom from shame. For this reason, we should unashamedly proclaim the Gospel and share the message of God's grace and love with those around us. Receiving God's grace ourselves is the catalyst for us being released from shame and therefore being able to accept others in the love of God, no matter what they have done in their past. We are a people who have been forgiven and made righteous. Refusing to receive shame demonstrates our belief in who we are as believers and releases us into a life of great exploits for the kingdom of God!

# STUDY QUESTIONS

1. When did Jesus become a shame substitute for us? ______________________

______________________________________________

______________________________________________

2. When you live a lifestyle of believing on Jesus and His finished works, you will

______________________________________________.

3. What are several sources of shame? ______________________

______________________________________________

4. What are three proactive steps to combat shame? ______________________

______________________________________________

______________________________________________

5. How do we renew our minds? ______________________

______________________________________________

______________________________________________

______________________________________________

6. When you despise shame, you refuse to allow it to ______________________

______________________________________.

7. How do you banish shame? ______________________________

______________________________________________________

8. God's ______________________ and ______________________ will overcome all shame.

9. True or False: The Gospel is the reason we can be free from shame.

10. ______________________________________ is a catalyst for us being free from shame and not shaming others.

# ANSWER KEY

1. when He offered Himself as a sacrifice for our sins
2. reject the voice of shame
3. accidents; victimization; inherited shame
4. despise it, banish it, and reject it
5. by finding Scriptures that relate to our situation and meditating on them until they change the way we think
6. influence your identity
7. Don't let it influence your actions toward others.
8. eternal love; honor
9. True
10. Receiving God's grace ourselves

## SCRIPTURE REFERENCES

Ezra 9:5-6
Isaiah 50:6-7
Psalm 139:14
Micah 7:19
Philippians 3:13
Hebrews 12:2
Romans 10:11
Romans 1:16

# CONCLUSION

It takes time for people to really get the revelation of the grace of God. It's a lifetime process of learning the Gospel and reevaluating everything you've been taught since you've been a Christian. Look back over it again and allow the grace of God to really bring the correct balance in your life. Ask yourself, "How does grace reconcile my understanding of this?" Your family, your finances, the fruit of the spirit, prayer—grace changes how you approach all of these things. Grace changes how you approach life.

I believe this message of grace because it *is* Jesus Christ. As we share this Gospel, lives are going to be changed. People will never be the same again. There's a freedom that comes when you experience and bathe in the grace of God. There's no more fear. There's no more lack. There's no more being in bondage to people. You walk around expecting unearned favor because you're a child of God! You understand that the requirements of the old covenant are not requirements of the new covenant. You walk around with a high and a good opinion of God, and of yourself in Him. You have a God-consciousness. Let me sum it up for you: You have Jesus!

His grace is sufficient for you, so walk in this freedom. Enjoy it! It's not a freedom to sin, but a freedom to walk like Jesus. *If* you sin, though, you have an advocate with the Father. Right in the middle of it, say, "I am *still* the righteousness of God! I am *still* redeemed! I am *still* sanctified! I am *still* holy!" Guess what happens? Your identity will change whatever behavior needs to be changed. Don't let your behavior change your identity. Make sure your identity keeps your behavior in check. All is well with you. All is well with your house. All is well with your marriage. All is well with your family. All is well with your finances. All. Is. Well!

# ABOUT THE AUTHOR

Creflo Dollar was born and raised in College Park, Georgia. He attended West Georgia College where he began World Changers Bible Study in his dorm room, and graduated in 1984 with a B.S. in educational therapy. Today, with his wife, Creflo pastors over 30,000 members at WCCI-College Park, World Changers Church-New York, and over 25 fellowship churches worldwide. WCCI also has offices on five continents.

Recognized for his cutting-edge revelation and humorous, pragmatic approach, Creflo empowers millions to experience God's grace, restoration, healing, and financial breakthrough by delivering simple, biblical principles to apply in their daily lives. Creflo is a world-renowned Bible teacher, best-selling author, and sought-after conference speaker with hundreds of books, CDs, and DVDs in worldwide distribution. He publishes CHANGE online magazine, and his award-winning television show, *Changing Your World*, is broadcast throughout the world and translated into six languages. His weekly teachings reach over 2 billion homes.

To further his goal of making a mark in lives that can never be erased, Creflo oversees the Creflo Dollar Ministerial Association, a "pool of resources" for ministries worldwide, as well as Creflo Dollar Global Missions, the outreach extension of his ministry.

Creflo and his wife, Taffi, have five children and live in Atlanta, Georgia.